D1742364

Science Directions

Year 3

Teaching File

Published by HarperCollins*Publishers* Limited
77–85 Fulham Palace Road
Hammersmith
London
W6 8JB

www.CollinsEducation.com
On-line support for schools and colleges

© HarperCollins*Publishers* Limited
First published 2000 Reprinted 2001 (twice)

18

ISBN-13 978 0 00 317 2546
ISBN-10 0 00 317 2546

Based on a scheme of work known as 'Science 3–11' developed and
provided by Suffolk County Council.

Chris Sunley and Jane Bourne assert the moral right to be identified
as the authors of this work.

All rights reserved. No part of this publication may be
reproduced, stored in a retrieval system, or transmitted in any
form or by any means, electronic, mechanical, photocopying,
recording or otherwise, without either the prior permission of
the Publisher or a licence permitting restricted copying in the
United Kingdom issued by the Copyright Licensing Agency Ltd.,
90 Tottenham Court Road, London W1P 9HE.

British Library Cataloguing in Publication Data
A catalogue record for this publication is available from the
British Library

Illustrations by Tim Oliver in association with
Cambridge Publishing Management
Design and Production by Cambridge Publishing Management

Printed by Martins the Printers Ltd.

Mixed Sources
Product group from well-managed
forests and other controlled sources
www.fsc.org   Cert no. SW-COC-1806
© 1996 Forest Stewardship Council
FSC

Contents

Introduction

Science Directions is a comprehensive and detailed scheme for pupils aged 3–11. It complies completely with the requirements of the Foundation Stage as specified in the Early Learning Goals, and with the Science National Curriculum programmes of study for Key Stages 1 and 2. Science Directions is also matched to the exemplar schemes of work produced by the Qualifications and Curriculum Authority (QCA). Moreover, the time allocations and titles of Science Directions units mirror those in the QCA scheme of work.

Science Directions has a straight-forward structure, comprising one Teaching File and one Pupil Book in each school year from Years 1 to 6. For each unit of work, the Teaching File provides detailed teachers' notes covering a range of activities. Some of the activities are drawn from the QCA schemes of work, others are new and extend the range of experiences for pupils.

Aims

The aims of Science Directions can be summarised as follows:

For Pupils

- to provide a rich and stimulating scientific experience which will foster fascination and interest in science;
- to present science as an essentially practical experience, based largely on first-hand experiences in relevant contexts;
- to develop investigative approaches to scientific enquiry which build confidence in tackling problems with increasing levels of independence;
- to encourage discussion of scientific ideas, and the abilities to question and justify;
- to support a sense of scientific curiosity and the development of appropriate levels of knowledge and understanding.

For Teachers

- to provide an accessible framework of advice and information which closely integrates teacher and pupil material;
- to link the National Curriculum programmes of study to appropriate and interesting activities with a range of possible pupil outcomes;
- to support continuity and progression between different years and key stages, and encourage a constructivist approach in which new ideas are developed from existing ones;
- to encourage the use of questioning to clarify, consolidate and extend understanding;

- to provide explicit links between the activities and National Curriculum levels of attainment, so that assessment of pupil progress can be on-going and informative;
- to support teachers by providing background information on the underlying scientific ideas and principles being developed.

Organisation of the Teaching File

The teaching file includes:

- detailed teacher notes for each unit;
- a set of photocopiable masters for each unit.

Each unit is set out in the following way.

Introductory page of the Unit

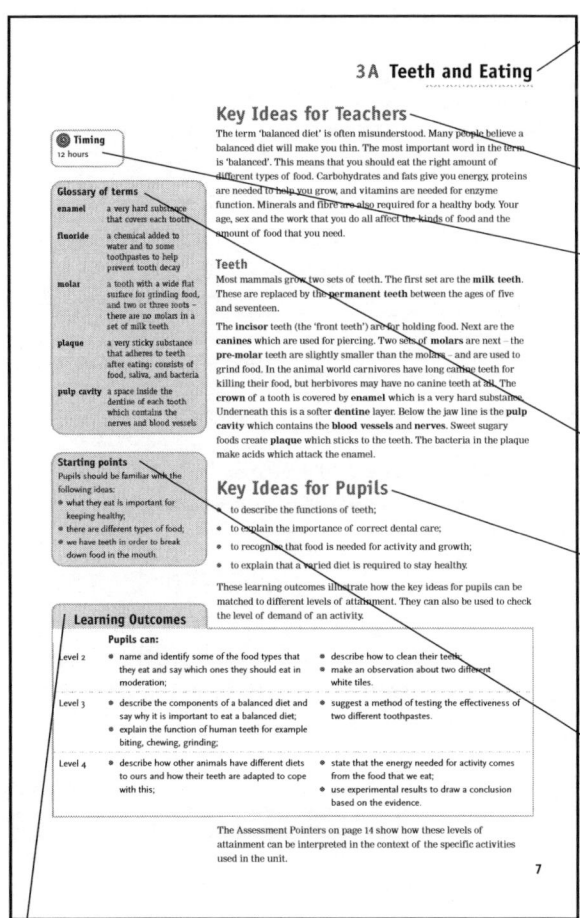

Unit reference and title which matches the QCA scheme of work for science exactly.

Useful background information for Teachers.

The approximate time needed for teaching the unit, based on the recommendations in the QCA scheme of work.

Clear explanations for teachers of key scientific terms relevant to the unit.

Ideas and concepts to be developed which relate directly to the National Curriculum programmes of study for Key Stage 2.

Ideas that pupils will have encountered through their Science Directions work in Key Stage 1.

Typical expectations of pupil attainment for the unit, including those for Sc1 and linked to National Curriculum levels.

Unit Activities

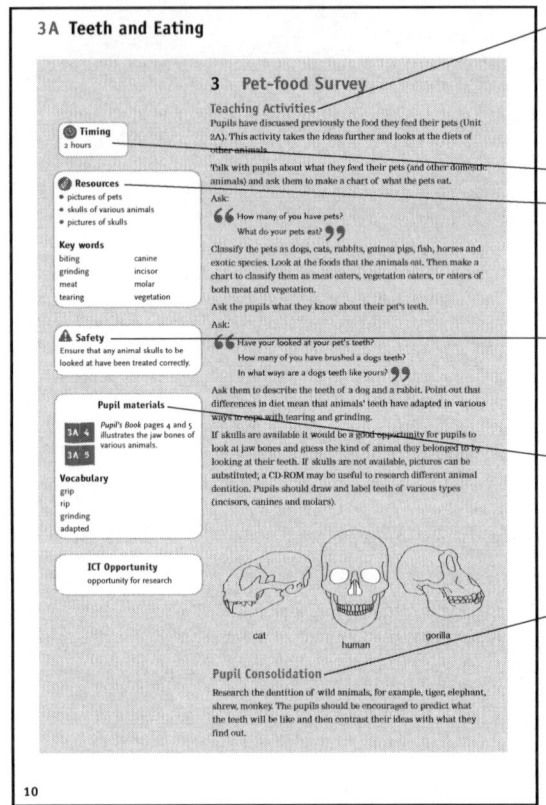

Detailed guidance on how to organise and sequence the various activities. Particular emphasis is given to questions which challenge pupils' thinking and ideas.

The approximate time to cover the activities.

A summary of resources needed and the Key Words that pupils should be introduced to during the activities.

Safety issues specific to the activities. Teachers should always make a risk assessment for the particular group of pupils they are teaching.

Reference to photocopiable masters and pages in the Pupil Book which relate directly to these activities. A summary of each pupil page is given to aid clarity.

Suggestions of other tasks and activities that the pupils can be given to consolidate their learning. In many cases the activities will tend to broaden and extend understanding. As such, they are more likely to be used with selected groups of pupils than with the whole class.

The Key Activity

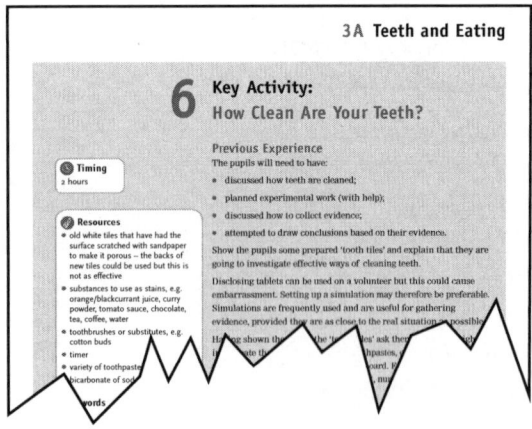

An activity which allows pupils to demonstrate their knowledge, skills and understanding of the unit.

This is usually the final activity in the unit. In almost all cases it provides a specific opportunity to develop and practise Sc1 investigative skills. If required, the activity can also be used to assess pupils' progress in Sc1.

End-of-unit Assessment

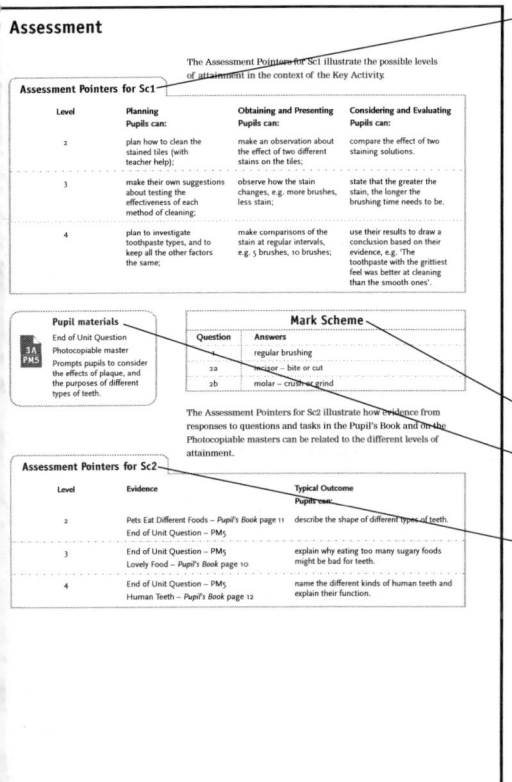

Possible learning outcomes for the Key Activity are provided, as well as some of those given on the first page of the unit. To simplify the assessment process, the learning outcomes are arranged under the 'strands' of planning; obtaining and presenting; considering and evaluating. The outcomes have been written to relate directly to the particular context of the Key Activity and include the type of response expected at each level of attainment. They are not exhaustive and so there will be many other acceptable responses.

Answers to the questions in the end-of-unit test.

Reference to one of the photocopiable masters which can be used as an end-of-unit test.

Indicators of attainment related to the learning outcomes given at the beginning of the unit, placed in the context of questions from the Pupil Book and photocopiable masters. Thus by looking back through the pupil's work, it should be possible to match the work to an overall level of attainment for the unit.

Approaches to Assessment

Science Directions has been designed on the premise that regular assessment of pupil attainment is desirable, and associated feedback to pupils on their progress is important. This does not mean that every piece of work needs to be assessed against National Curriculum levels of attainment. However, if end-of-year judgements are to be made in relation to National Curriculum levels, it is sensible for interim judgements to be carried out similarly.

The approach suggested is to identify certain 'pointers' in each unit which relate to particular 'significant activities', that is, activities which have learning outcomes indicative of a pupil's level of knowledge, understanding or investigative skills. For example, the Key Activity can be seen as a significant activity as it lends itself to the assessment of Sc1. In addition, certain questions in the Pupil Book and on the photocopiable masters can be used as good indicators of levels of attainment.

As judgements on individual pupils are made unit by unit, a profile of attainment emerges and can be established. It is then easy at the end of the year to make an overall judgement on pupil attainment.

A more detailed rationale of the assessment approach, and further advice, can be found in the Co-ordinator's Handbook.

The Pupil Book

Drawings and Photographs

Illustrations are used extensively, not only to convey information, but also to stimulate interest and show the relevance of the scientific ideas being considered.

They should provide a stimulus for discussion and questioning, both with individuals and the class as a whole.

Questions

Questions at the bottom of the page relate directly to the information on the single or double page. Generally the later questions are harder than the earlier ones. They can be used as a basis for whole class discussion or for individual or small group work.

Remember box

This box includes the key facts and ideas that the pupils should be able to recall.

 **Timing**

12 hours

Glossary of terms

enamel	a very hard substance that covers each tooth
fluoride	a chemical added to water and to some toothpastes to help prevent tooth decay
molar	a tooth with a wide flat surface for grinding food, and two or three roots – there are no molars in a set of milk teeth
plaque	a very sticky substance that adheres to teeth after eating: consists of food, saliva, and bacteria
pulp cavity	a space inside the dentine of each tooth which contains the nerves and blood vessels

Starting points

Pupils should be familiar with the following ideas:
* what they eat is important for keeping healthy;
* there are different types of food;
* we have teeth in order to break down food in the mouth.

Key Ideas for Teachers

The term 'balanced diet' is often misunderstood. Many people believe a balanced diet will make you thin. The most important word in the term is 'balanced'. This means that you should eat the right amount of different types of food. Carbohydrates and fats give you energy, proteins are needed to help you grow, and vitamins are needed for enzyme function. Minerals and fibre are also required for a healthy body. Your age, sex and the work that you do all affect the kinds of food and the amount of food that you need.

Teeth

Most mammals grow two sets of teeth. The first set are the **milk teeth**. These are replaced by the **permanent teeth** between the ages of five and seventeen.

The **incisor** teeth (the 'front teeth') are for holding food. Next are the **canines** which are used for piercing. Two sets of **molars** are next – the **pre-molar** teeth are slightly smaller than the molars – and are used to grind food. In the animal world carnivores have long canine teeth for killing their food, but herbivores may have no canine teeth at all. The **crown** of a tooth is covered by **enamel** which is a very hard substance. Underneath this is a softer **dentine** layer. Below the jaw line is the **pulp cavity** which contains the **blood vessels** and **nerves**. Sweet sugary foods create **plaque** which sticks to the teeth. The bacteria in the plaque make acids which attack the enamel.

Key Ideas for Pupils

* to describe the functions of teeth;
* to explain the importance of correct dental care;
* to recognise that food is needed for activity and growth;
* to explain that a varied diet is required to stay healthy.

These learning outcomes illustrate how the key ideas for pupils can be matched to different levels of attainment. They can also be used to check the level of demand of an activity.

Learning Outcomes

Pupils can:

Level 2	• name and identify some of the food types that they eat and say which ones they should eat in moderation;	• describe how to clean their teeth; • make an observation about two different white tiles.
Level 3	• describe the components of a balanced diet and say why it is important to eat a balanced diet; • explain the function of human teeth for example biting, chewing, grinding;	• suggest a method of testing the effectiveness of two different toothpastes.
Level 4	• describe how other animals have different diets to ours and how their teeth are adapted to cope with this;	• state that the energy needed for activity comes from the food that we eat; • use experimental results to draw a conclusion based on the evidence.

The Assessment Pointers on page 14 show how these levels of attainment can be interpreted in the context of the specific activities used in the unit.

Timing

2 hours

Resources

- clean empty food packaging
- supermarket visit (optional)

Key words

diet	energy
fibre	fresh
frozen	growth
health	minerals
tinned	vitamins

Safety

If you are able to take pupils out to a supermarket check local school and LEA guidelines.

Pupil materials

3A 2 **3A** 3	Pupil's Book pages 2 and 3 prompt pupils to examine ways of packaging foods.

Vocabulary

'on display'
occasionally
equal
variety
amounts

1   Supermarket Survey

Teaching Activities

Pupils will construct a virtual greengrocers in unit 3B on plant life. The emphasis here is on supermarkets and different food types. While it does not preclude fruits and vegetables, the focus is food groups.

Go over what pupils remember about food in unit 2A 'Health and Growth'. Ask them to tell each other the types of foods they like and dislike eating. Ask:

 Do you eat any foods that you don't really like, but feel you ought to?

The answer is probably yes because they are good for you. Explore with the class what 'good for you' means.

A visit to a supermarket would be useful to look at how food is stored and set out. If a visit is not possible ask the pupils to set out the classroom like a typical supermarket. Allow them to move the desks to make aisles, and use paper representations or clean packaging for the various food types.

Ask the pupils:

 Why are all the tinned foods on the same aisle?

How many different ways of packaging foods can you think of?

Explain that foods can be assigned to various groups depending on what they contain.

Give the pupils these groups: meats and fish; cereals; sweets; drinks; fruit and vegetables (fibre). Ask them to re-sort the room into these categories. Explain that each food type does a different job in the body: meat and fish for growth; cereals and sweet things for energy and activity; drinks are essential to keep the body healthy; fruits and vegetables provide essential vitamins, minerals and fibre.

2 Diet Does Not Mean Thin

Timing
2 hours

Key words
diet   exercise
healthy   lifestyle

Pupil materials

3A PM1

Photocopiable master provides a blank menu for pupils to fill in.

Teaching Activities

Following the supermarket survey the pupils should discuss what they understand by the term 'balanced diet' and come up with five features of a balanced diet, which they should write down.

Ask the pupils:

 What do we mean by a 'balanced diet'?

'Does eating a balanced diet mean that you should not eat chocolate?'

Divide the class into groups to share ideas and to look at similarities on their lists; how many of the pupils picked out sweet things as a feature? Stress at this point that 'diet' does not equate to slimming and that people have different dietary requirements depending on their age and lifestyle.

Ask:

 How many of you put fruit and vegetables on your lists?

How many put chips and biscuits on the list?

In pairs the pupils should design a menu for a 'Healthy party'. Give the class the following instructions:

- **Context:** This party is to be held at the local swimming pool and then at the pupil's house.

- **Conditions:** They can have any foods that they wish and it should be as appetising as possible.

- **Points to bear in mind:** Remind them that they will have been taking exercise first and possibly dancing afterwards.

The suggested menu proforma is provided on photocopiable master 3A PM1.

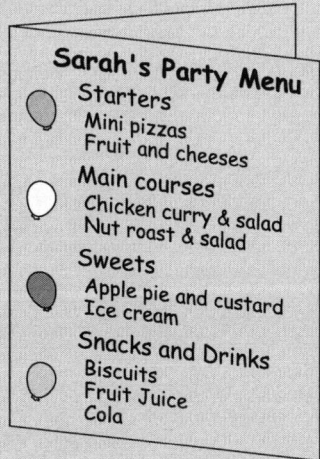

Timing

2 hours

Resources

- pictures of pets
- skulls of various animals
- pictures of skulls

Key words

biting	canine
grinding	incisor
meat	molar
tearing	vegetation

Safety

Ensure that any animal skulls to be looked at have been treated correctly.

Pupil materials

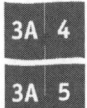

3A	4
3A	5

Pupil's Book pages 4 and 5 illustrates the jaw bones of various animals.

Vocabulary

grip

rip

grinding

adapted

ICT Opportunity

opportunity for research

3 Pet-food Survey

Teaching Activities

Pupils have discussed previously the food they feed their pets (Unit 2A). This activity takes the ideas further and looks at the diets of other animals.

Talk with pupils about what they feed their pets (and other domestic animals) and ask them to make a chart of what the pets eat.

Ask:

 How many of you have pets?

What do your pets eat?

Classify the pets as dogs, cats, rabbits, guinea pigs, fish, horses and exotic species. Look at the foods that the animals eat. Then make a chart to classify them as meat eaters, vegetation eaters, or eaters of both meat and vegetation.

Ask the pupils what they know about their pet's teeth.

Ask:

 Have your looked at your pet's teeth?

How many of you have brushed a dogs teeth?

In what ways are a dogs teeth like yours?

Ask them to describe the teeth of a dog and a rabbit. Point out that differences in diet mean that animals' teeth have adapted in various ways to cope with tearing and grinding.

If skulls are available it would be a good opportunity for pupils to look at jaw bones and guess the kind of animal they belonged to by looking at their teeth. If skulls are not available, pictures can be substituted; a CD-ROM may be useful to research different animal dentition. Pupils should draw and label teeth of various types (incisors, canines and molars).

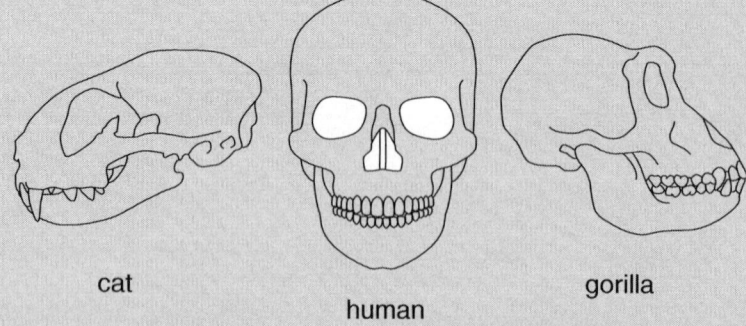

cat

human

gorilla

Pupil Consolidation

Research the dentition of wild animals, for example, tiger, elephant, shrew, monkey. The pupils should be encouraged to predict what the teeth will be like and then contrast their ideas with what they find out.

4 Teeth

 **Timing**
2 hours

 **Resources**
- dental mirrors (available from most chemists)
- large drawing of teeth
- samples of sterilised teeth

Key words

enamel   milk teeth

permanent teeth

 Safety
Make sure that old teeth and dental mirrors are sterilised before examination.

Pupil materials

3A 6 — Pupil's Book page 6 illustrates the teeth in a human jaw.

Vocabulary
regularly
last (verb)

Teaching Activities
Ask the class how they keep their teeth healthy.

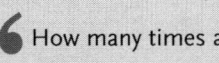 *How many times a day do you brush your teeth?*

Their answers should include brushing them with toothpaste, going to the dentist and possibly taking fluoride drops. Using a mirror, ask the pupils to count how many teeth they have. This will vary depending on how many they have lost!

Tell them that the majority of pupils have 20 milk teeth and these are replaced by 32 permanent teeth which will not regrow if they are lost.

Give the pupils a dental mirror and ask them to look carefully at a friend's teeth. See if they can tell the difference between the types of teeth.

Ask:

Who has been to the dentist recently?
Did your dentist use a mirror like this one?

Show the pupils a large drawing of the various kinds of teeth and ask them to draw the teeth.

Show a model of the human jaw and point out the kinds of teeth in the adult mouth.

Explain that the tooth is covered by a very strong substance called enamel that helps to protect what is inside the tooth and also provides a good surface for biting and grinding.

Pupils may wish to bring old teeth in from home. These must be sterilised before use in the classroom. Dental suppliers are usually willing to provide samples for pupils to examine.

Pupil Consolidation
The school dental nurse could be invited in to demonstrate the correct care of teeth.

Note: Dental professionals are often tempted to show pupils a cross section of a tooth including nerves and blood supply, but this can be confusing and it is better to concentrate on external, observable features.

3A Teeth and Eating

Timing

2 hours

Resources

- tooth that has been soaked in a fizzy drink
- hand lenses
- mock tooth cut out of expanded polystyrene
- nail varnish remover (acetone based). Caution: this is flammable and should only be used by the teacher and in a well-ventilated room
- chicken bone
- vinegar

Key words

acid	bacteria
brushing	calcium
plaque	sweet

Pupil materials

Photocopiable master provides a format for producing a leaflet.

Pupil's Book pages 8 and 9 discuss the merits of regular teeth brushing.

Vocabulary

saliva

decay

substance

5 Healthy Gums

Teaching Activities

Ask pupils to remember what they do in order to keep their teeth healthy. Show them a tooth that has been in cola or some other fizzy drink overnight.

Ask:

 Can you see anything covering the surface of the tooth?

What do you think it is?

Who knows what plaque is?

Explain that there are bacteria in the mouth, too small to be visible. Tell the class that this is normal, that the bacteria like to 'eat' sweet things, but they produce an acid.

Refer back to the tooth in the fizzy drink and explain that the covering is a mixture of food, bacteria and acid.

The acid can eat away at the enamel on the teeth and gums and cause tooth decay.

Ask:

 How many times a day do you drink fizzy pop?

You can demonstrate this effect of tooth decay with the following model:

- Take a piece of expanded polystyrene and cut it into the shape of a tooth.

- In a well-ventilated room, carefully drop small quantities of nail varnish remover onto it. The pupils will see the nail varnish remover 'eat' into the polystyrene causing it to fragment.

- Explain that this is a model of what happens in the mouth if plaque is not removed by regular brushing.

Another way to demonstrate is to keep a clean chicken leg bone in vinegar for a couple of days, then remove and dry it. Show it to the pupils and explain that the acid has attacked some of the chemicals in the bone and made it soft.

The chemical in teeth and bones is calcium. Link this to the earlier work on minerals required for a healthy diet.

As a result of these demonstrations, and other research, the pupils should be able to produce a leaflet, designed for a specific audience, e.g. teenagers, to warn people about dental decay. The Photocopiable master 3APM2 provides a format for this.

Pupil Consolidation

Groups should prepare a presentation, using visual aids, to encourage other/older pupils to care for their permanent teeth as these cannot be replaced.

6 Key Activity:
How Clean Are Your Teeth?

Timing
2 hours

Resources
- old white tiles that have had the surface scratched with sandpaper to make it porous – the backs of new tiles could be used but this is not as effective
- substances to use as stains, e.g. orange/blackcurrant juice, curry powder, tomato sauce, chocolate, tea, coffee, water
- toothbrushes or substitutes, e.g. cotton buds
- timer
- variety of toothpastes
- bicarbonate of soda

Key words

brushes	compare
effective	fair test
plan	record
time	results

Safety
As with all food substances used in the classroom the pupils must be warned not to taste the items and not to put them near the eyes (curry powder especially).

Pupil materials

Photocopiable master provides a mock-up letter from a toothpaste manufacturer.

Photocopiable master provides a writing frame for the pupils to plan their investigation.

Previous Experience
The pupils will need to have:

- discussed how teeth are cleaned;
- planned experimental work (with help);
- discussed how to collect evidence;
- attempted to draw conclusions based on their evidence.

Show the pupils some prepared 'tooth tiles' and explain that they are going to investigate effective ways of cleaning teeth.

Discolouring tablets can be used on a volunteer but this could cause embarrassment. Setting up a simulation may therefore be preferable. Simulations are frequently used and are useful for gathering evidence, provided they are as close to the real situation as possible.

Having shown the pupils the 'tooth tiles' ask them how they might investigate the effects of different toothpastes, or ways of brushing. Gather the pupils' suggestions on the board. Fair testing is important. For example, keeping the staining agent, numbers of brushes and types of toothpaste constant. Discuss:

- how they are going to be fair with their brushing, i.e. how will they ensure the same vigour of brushing?
- how they will keep the amount of staining agent the same; what mass, or number of spoonfuls?
- how they will keep the amount of toothpaste constant: 0.5 cm?

After discussion ask the pupils to plan the investigation: Photocopiable master 3APM3 will help set the scene; Photocopiable master 3APM4 will help them organise their ideas.

After planning, pupils should carry out the investigation and collect evidence. This should be used to write a report to the local dental clinic outlining their findings, and making recommendations for the dentists to pass on to patients.

Assessment

The Assessment Pointers for Sc1 illustrate the possible levels of attainment in the context of the Key Activity.

Assessment Pointers for Sc1

Level	Planning Pupils can:	Obtaining and Presenting Pupils can:	Considering and Evaluating Pupils can:
2	plan how to clean the stained tiles (with teacher help);	make an observation about the effect of two different stains on the tiles;	compare the effect of two staining solutions.
3	make their own suggestions about testing the effectiveness of each method of cleaning;	observe how the stain changes, e.g. more brushes, less stain;	state that the greater the stain, the longer the brushing time needs to be.
4	plan to investigate toothpaste types, and to keep all the other factors the same;	make comparisons of the stain at regular intervals, e.g. 5 brushes, 10 brushes;	use their results to draw a conclusion based on their evidence, e.g. 'The toothpaste with the grittiest feel was better at cleaning than the smooth ones'.

Pupil materials

End of Unit Question

Photocopiable master

Prompts pupils to consider the effects of plaque, and the purposes of different types of teeth.

Mark Scheme

Question	Answers
1	regular brushing
2a	incisor – bite or cut
2b	molar – crush or grind

The Assessment Pointers for Sc2 illustrate how evidence from responses to questions and tasks in the Pupil's Book and on the Photocopiable masters can be related to the different levels of attainment.

Assessment Pointers for Sc2

Level	Evidence	Typical Outcome Pupils can:
2	Pets Eat Different Foods – Pupil's Book page 5 End of Unit Question – PM5	describe the shape of different types of teeth.
3	End of Unit Question – PM5 Lovely Food – Pupil's Book page 3	explain why eating too many sugary foods might be bad for teeth.
4	End of Unit Question – PM5 Human Teeth – Pupil's Book page 6	name the different kinds of human teeth and explain their function.

Key Ideas for Teachers

It was established in Key Stage 1 that plants manufacture their own food using chemicals. This process is called photosynthesis. Two chemicals are needed; carbon dioxide and water. These chemicals are changed into sugar (glucose) and oxygen by a chemical reaction in the plant. Energy is required to make the reaction work, and this comes from sunlight. The sunlight is trapped by a chemical in the leaves called chlorophyll.

Some of the sugar made by this process is used by the plant for respiration which provides energy for the plant cells. Minerals are also required to make new cells. These minerals are absorbed from the soil by the roots of the plant. These minerals are often referred to as food: this is incorrect, the plant makes its own food.

Key Ideas for Pupils

- that plant growth is affected by light, air and the availability of water and temperature;

- the root anchors the plant in the soil, and this is where the plant takes up water and minerals. These are then transported through the stem to other parts of the plant;

- the leaf produces new materials in order for the plant to grow.

Timing

12 hours

Glossary of terms

chlorophyll   the green chemical found in structures in the leaves (chloroplasts) which gives leaves their colour, and which traps the sunlight energy

mineral salts   chemical substances which are found in soil in very small quantities

photosynthesis   the process by which plants manufacture food. Carbon dioxide, water, energy (from sunlight) and chlorophyll are needed to make sugar

Starting points

Pupils should be familiar with the following ideas:
- parts of a plant from Key Stage 1, e.g. leaf, stem, root;
- that plants need water to grow;
- plants are living things and should be treated with care. Also, that it is an offence to pick wild flowers.

These learning outcomes illustrate how the key ideas for pupils can be matched to different levels of attainment. They can also be used to check the level of demand of an activity.

Learning Outcomes

Pupils can:

Level 2	• state that plants require light and water to grow;	• rank plants in order from tallest to shortest.
Level 3	• explain that plants provide food for humans, and that different parts of a plant can be eaten;	• describe how plants need the right amount of water, light and warmth in order for them to grow well; • make measurements of plant growth.
Level 4	• describe the effect of lack of water or light on plant growth; • simply describe the function of the roots and stem;	• make connections between the way in which plants are grown, the height and condition of the plant.

The Assessment Pointers on page 22 show how these levels of attainment can be interpreted in the context of the specific activities used in the unit.

1 Virtual Greengrocers

Teaching Activities

Talk to the pupils about the things they could buy in a greengrocer's (or supermarket). List all the items that they suggest, for example, cabbage, potatoes, fruit such as apples, oranges, grapes etc. Make the list as long as possible, and include exotic fruit and vegetables.

Talk about the items that they have listed and ask the pupils to identify which parts of the plant they would eat.

Ask:

 Which part of a plant do you eat?

Then ask the class to make life-sized drawings of as many of the fruits and vegetables as they can and display them in trays, just like a real greengrocer would.

The display can then be used throughout this unit of work. The virtual fruits and vegetables (drawings and models) should be labelled with stem, shoot, root, flower, leaf to show parts of plants that can be eaten.

If funds allow, real examples could be displayed, although they are likely to decay before the end of the unit.

Pupil Consolidation

Set the pupils the task of completing a survey of the plants discussed earlier, collecting data on the number of species from which we eat roots, leaves, stems and flowers. They should present their findings on a bar chart to show which is the most popular part of the plant to eat.

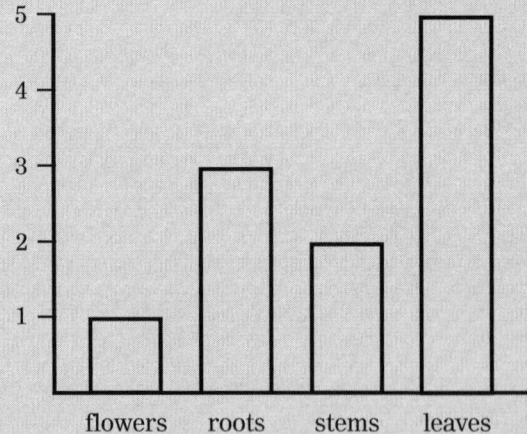

Timing

2 hours

Resources

- pictures or real examples of a range of fruit and vegetables
- drawing or modelling materials to make fruits and vegetables

Key words

names of fruits and vegetables

eat	flower
leaf	stem
root	dispersed

Pupil materials

3B 10
3B 11

Pupil's Book pages 10 and 11 instruct pupils to make a chart of roots and shoots etc. of plants that are eaten.

Vocabulary

attracts (verb)

ICT Opportunity

opportunity to use a data handling programme

---

2 The Structure of Plants

Teaching Activities

Using a real plant introduce the idea that it is a living organism, and that each part of it does a different job.

Ask the pupils:

> How do we know this plant is living?
> What job do you think the leaves do?

Contrast the plant structure with human body parts and functions: legs for running, teeth for chewing.

Ask the pupils what job they think the leaves do. Show them a number of plants of the same species, for example, geraniums, and ask them how they would find out if the plant needed its leaves in order to grow well.

> How can we find out if the leaves of this plant are needed in order for it to grow?

Using their ideas set up an experiment using plants with different numbers of leaves and plot their growth and state of health.

The plants should have between one and lots of leaves. Ask:

> How will we judge how healthy the plant is?

Gather their ideas and build up an 'index of health' for the plants, e.g. colour of leaves, how droopy the plant is, colour of the stem.

Ask:

> What do you think would happen to a plant if we tried to grow it without its roots?

Establish that the roots are needed to anchor the plant and are used to transport water to the rest of the plant.

The pupils should write up a method for the experiment, and make predictions about which plants they think will grow the best and be the healthiest, e.g. 'I think the plant with lots of leaves will grow the best because they help the plant make food.'

Encourage them to think about making their experiment fair, for example, watering with the same volume of water, keeping the plants in the same conditions of light and warmth.

⏱ Timing

2 hours

✏ Resources

- plants in flower, e.g. geraniums

Key words

growth	healthy
leaf	light
variegated	water

Pupil materials

3B PM1 Photocopiable master provides a recording sheet for the plant growth experiment.

3B 11 Pupil's Book page 11 explains what each part of a plant does.

3 The Root as a Special Organ

Teaching Activities

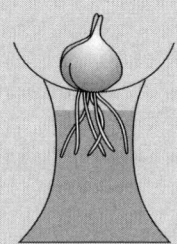

Resources
- bulb in a clear container
- celery (with leaves and roots)
- food colouring
- knife
- rulers

Key words

amount	bulb
shoots	roots
veins	
food colouring (dye)	

Use the display from Activity 1 and list all the plants whose roots we eat, e.g. potato, parsnip, carrot.

Show the pupils a bulb in a clear container with the roots dipping into water.

Ask:

> How much water do you think a plant takes in through its roots in a week?

Gather their ideas, which might include: marking the level of water on the side of the jar; measuring the mass etc.

Ask a group of pupils to find out how much water the bulb needs in a week. If resources allow, arrange for all pupils to do the experiment. They will probably measure the amount the water levels drop with a ruler, and mark this on the side of the jar.

Show the pupils a stick of celery – ideally one with lots of leaves and some roots still attached. Let them examine the celery and describe its structure. Point out the veins going up the shoots.

Take a stick of celery from near the centre of the plant, take off the roots and split the stem in two, placing each half in dyed water. Two different colours will have a more spectacular effect.

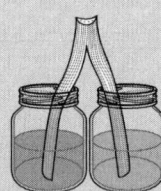

Leave the celery for about half an hour and then let the pupils examine it. In the meantime ask the pupils what they think will happen to the dye. They can draw or write about their predictions. Slice across the stem horizontally to get a cross section of the stalk. You should be able to see the dye in the veins of the plant. Conclude by explaining that the root takes in the water which is carried to the rest of the plant through the veins in the stem and eventually reaches the leaves, where it is used in photosynthesis.

Pupil Consolidation

Using a number of stems of celery, calculate how far the dye rises up the stem after 10 mins, 20 mins, 30 mins.

4 Key Activity:
Greenhouse Investigation

Previous Experience:

Refer back to the display produced in Activity 1, Virtual Greengrocers, and ask the pupils:

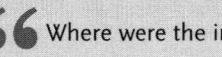 Where were the individual plants grown?

List all the places such as fields, pots etc.

Explain that they are going to investigate what happens to plants grown in a greenhouse. A light bank, or clear plastic bottle base used as a cloche, can easily substitute greenhouse conditions.

Ask the pupils:

 What conditions are present in the greenhouse, for example, light, warmth, air and water?

Show the pupils some radish seeds and explain that the investigation is about what conditions these seeds need in order to grow into healthy radishes.

The radishes are to be grown in empty film canisters and the pupils should decide on the conditions that they want to investigate.

Assign small groups of pupils to investigate different conditions: limit them to one as there are so many variables in this investigation.

Remind them about fair testing and let them plan their investigation – Photocopiable master 3BPM2 can be used here.

Encourage the pupils to plant more than one seed, as using just one may lead to odd results.

The pupils should decide how to measure their seeds' progress, for example, height of growth, change in mass. They should record the progress of their seeds over the next two weeks (say every two days).

Pupil Consolidation

Using CD-ROMs or books, research plants growing in different climates. Look for how they are adapted to do this, for example, through water-retaining stems on a cactus, tiny leaves on plants that live in very cold areas.

⏱ Timing
2 hours

✏ Resources
- radish seeds
- empty film canisters
- growing medium (compost)
- water
- plastic bottles to make greenhouses
- measuring cylinders or syringes for measuring water
- thermometer
- ruler

Key words

amount	conditions
fair test	height
measure	warmth

Pupil materials

3B PM2 Photocopiable master provides a writing frame for planning the investigation.

3B 11 Pupil's Book page 11 illustrates the parts of a plant and their functions.

3B 14 Pupil's Book page 14 discusses growing seeds.

🖥 ICT Opportunity

opportunity for research

5 Keeping Plants in the Dark

Teaching Activities

Ask the pupils:

 What will happen to plants if we keep them in the dark?

Ask them to draw what they think a bean plant would look like if it was kept in the dark (they may remember growing beans in Key Stage 1 Unit 1B, Growing Plants).

Show some plants that have been kept in the dark and ask pupils to provide some descriptive words that would explain what the plant looks like, for example, yellow, thin, spindly (weedy).

Set up a demonstration using a bean plant.

Beans are ideal for showing the effects of light deprivation, because they grow quickly and exhibit pale colours and spindly stems.

Put a bean plant in a card box – the type that contains A4 paper is about the right size.

Make a maze for the plant to grow round then cut a hole in the top. The bean plant will grow towards the light and make its way around the maze to get there.

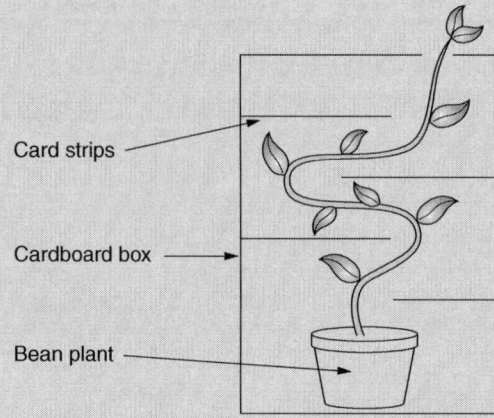

Card strips

Cardboard box

Bean plant

The pupils could also experiment by covering up areas of grass and looking at the effects of lack of light over time. Use black plastic bags to obtain a good effect.

Pupil Consolidation

Research the ingredients of 'plant food' products by looking at the labels. Explain that their plants have grown perfectly well without these products because the plant makes its own food. These products are chemicals that help different parts of the plant to grow – they are not food in the way in which animals need food to survive.

Timing
2 hours

Resources
- bean plant, e.g. runner or broad
- cardboard box
- strips of cardboard
- sticky tape
- black plastic bags – warn the pupils not to place the bags over their heads

⚠ Safety
Warn pupils that these plant products are chemicals and should be treated with caution.

Pupil materials

3B 12 **3B 13** Pupil's Book pages 12 and 13 illustrate how new plants are formed from seeds. They also provide pupils with a recipe for producing alfalfa toast.

6 Greenhouse Investigation Continued

Teaching Activities

Discuss with the class the results of their investigations.

Ask:

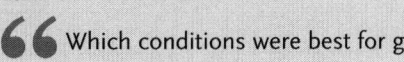

At this stage pupils often still believe that their plants grew the best, and will ignore the evidence.

Gather together the sets of radishes grown in different conditions in Activity 4. Rank them from tall to short. If some of the seedlings have been grown in the dark they are likely to be tall, but not very healthy: this point should be discussed with the pupils. If necessary, refer back to Activity 2 where the pupils produced an index of health for the plant. They should look for a good green colour – not yellow – and firm stems, not spindly ones.

Make a list of the conditions each of the plants were grown in and see if the pupils can come up with a list of rules for the successful growth of plants. Encourage them to measure the plants with a ruler and record the heights of growth. Discuss why not all plants in the same conditions grew the same amount. This will make the point that in science not all experimental results will be the same. Stress that plants are living things and, like humans, individual plants can grow to different heights. This is why it is necessary to plant more than one seed.

The pupils should use the results of their experiment to write a plant grower's guide for use by other pupils in the school. Photocopiable master 3BPM3 gives a format for this.

Pupil Consolidation

Some pupils will be able to calculate the average heights of the different groups of plants and plot them on a bar chart. They should be encouraged to write about possible sources of error in the experiment, for example, different amounts of water being used by different groups.

Timing

2 hours

Resources

- radishes from Activity 4
- rulers or some other means of measuring
- squared or graph paper

Key words

conditions	germination
growth	light
plants	seedlings
warm	wet

Pupil materials

 **3B PM2**

 3B PM3

Photocopiable masters provide frameworks for creating the plant grower's guide.

3B 12

Pupil's Book page 12 could be referred to in order to consolidate understanding of the life cycle of a plant.

 3B 16

3B 17

Pupil's Book pages 16 and 17 asks pupils to examine experimental evidence.

Vocabulary

caused

absorb

dissolve

Assessment

The Assessment Pointers for Sc1 illustrate the possible levels of attainment in the context of the Key Activity.

Assessment Pointers for Sc1

Level	Planning Pupils can:	Obtaining and Presenting Pupils can:	Considering and Evaluating Pupils can:
2	plan to draw how the plants are growing;	state which plants grew the tallest;	physically rank the sets of plants from tallest to shortest.
3	state that the heights of plants will need to be measured;	measure the heights of the plants with a ruler;	state which plants grew the best.
4	plan to take a series of measurements, e.g. heights, every two days;	accurately use a ruler to measure the heights of plants at regular intervals;	produce a general statement about the height the plants grew and the conditions in which they were grown.

Pupil materials

3B PM4

End of Unit Question
Photocopiable master asks what plants need to grow and how they obtain food.

Mark Scheme

Question	Answers
1	air, water
2	water through the roots mixes with sunlight falling on the leaf
3	roots take in water; roots anchor the plant

The Assessment Pointers for Sc2 illustrate how evidence from responses to questions and tasks in the Pupil's Book and on the Photocopiable masters can be related to the different levels of attainment.

Assessment Pointers for Sc2

Level	Evidence	Typical Outcome Pupils can:
2	Investigating Plant Growth – PM1	state that plants need light and water to grow.
3	Investigating Plant Growth – PM1 Growing Seeds – Pupil's Book page 15	describe the effect of lack of water on plant growth.
4	Plant Growers' Guide – PM2/3	state that a plant manufactures its own food.

Glossary of terms

electrical conductor	a material which allows the flow of an electric current
magnetic material	a material that is attracted to a magnet; one that can be magnetised
property	an attribute or quality belonging to something

Starting points

Pupils should be familiar with the following ideas:

- materials can be sorted into groups on the basis of simple properties;
- common types of material include metal, wood, plastic, paper and rock;
- materials can have different uses;
- the choice of material for a use depends on its properties.

Key Ideas for Teachers

A property of a material is simply a characteristic: size can be considered as a property. The key concept to be developed in this unit is the link between the property of a material and uses related to this property. In this context, size is rarely a helpful property to consider. Similarly, colour is not particularly helpful: it can be changed. The choice of material for a particular use will invariably be a compromise after consideration of a range of factors. For example, silver might be considered to be a better choice for electrical wiring than copper as it is a better electrical conductor. However, it is much more expensive than copper and so is not used for this purpose.

The melting point of a substance is an important property. In this unit the emphasis can be placed on questions such as 'Does it melt?'. It can be noted that chocolate and butter do return to their original state on cooling. A more detailed consideration of reversible and irreversible changes is included in Unit 6D.

Children are fascinated by some of the 'invisible' properties, such as magnetic properties and electrical conductivity. Of the 'everyday' metals, only iron (steel) and its alloys are magnetic. In contrast to this, all metals are electrical conductors. Graphite ('pencil lead', a form of carbon, a non-metal) is also an electrical conductor.

Key Ideas for Pupils

- to compare everyday materials, such as wood, rock, iron, aluminium, paper, polythene, on the basis of their properties, including hardness, strength, flexibility and magnetic behaviour, and to relate these properties to everyday uses of materials;
- that heating or cooling materials can cause them to change;
- that some changes can be reversed and some cannot.

These learning outcomes illustrate how the key ideas for pupils can be matched to different levels of attainment. They can also be used to check the level of demand of an activity.

Learning Outcomes

Pupils can:

Level 2	• sort a selection of materials using properties such as hardness, texture and transparency; • choose a material because it is able to do the job, for example, plastic for a rain hat because it will keep the rain off;	• make suggestions, with prompting, as to how a test can be carried out.
Level 3	• suggest several reasons why a material is suitable for a particular job; • understand why it is important to test materials when comparing certain properties, for example, strength;	• give a simple conclusion when considering evidence.
Level 4	• make predictions about whether changes can be reversed or not;	• explain how to make a fair test and use a bar chart to show results.

The Assessment Pointers on page 30 show how these levels of attainment can be interpreted in the context of the specific activities used in the unit.

3C Characteristics of Materials

1 Classifying Materials

Resources

- a wide range of materials including: wood, rock, iron/steel, paper, plastic (polythene), fabric
- some objects including: scissors, plastic/wooden ruler, hammer
- bar magnets

Key words

flexible	hardness
magnetic	property
transparent	

Safety

Pupils should not test computers or tape recorders with their magnets.

Pupil materials

3C PM1 — Photocopiable master prompts pupils to identify the material used to make various objects and say why the material has been chosen.

3C PM2 — Photocopiable master prompts pupils to identify materials and say why the material has been chosen.

3C 19 — Pupil's Book page 19 prompts pupils to identify the materials used to make the various parts of a bicycle and the property which makes it suitable.

Vocabulary
visor
attached

Teaching Activities

The purpose of this activity is to assess pupils' existing knowledge which can be developed in the rest of this unit.

Start with a selection of materials on a table and ask the pupils to suggest how they could be grouped. For example:

 Which of the materials are hard?

What word can we use that is the opposite to hard?

How else could we group the materials?

Encourage them to use classifications such as hard, soft, flexible (bendy), brittle (non-bendy), transparent (see through), non-transparent (opaque) and to use the word 'property'. Produce a word list of the properties. Ask the pupils which of the materials will be attracted to a magnet.

Divide the class into groups. Give each group a bar magnet and ask them to choose ten objects in the classroom: five objects which they think will be magnetic, and five which will be non-magnetic. To help ensure success, make sure there are a few magnetic objects clearly in view, such as steel scissors. Provide the pupils with a table (like that on Photocopiable master 3CPM1) to complete, and ask them to make their predictions before they start testing. When they have completed their testing ask them if they can see any pattern in their results.

Introduce the idea of a link between property and use.

 Why are these scissors made from steel?

Why are the window panes made from glass?

Ask the pupils to do a survey round the school of materials which have been used for particular purposes, for example, bricks for the walls. Ask them to complete a chart showing: material; what the material is used for; why the material is good for this use.

Pupil Consolidation

Ask the pupils to look at a drawing or photograph of a bicycle. They should then compile a table showing the parts of the bicycle, what each is made of and state why the material has been chosen.

Direct the pupils to make a list of the six objects used in the home. For each they should write down what the object is made from and why this material has been used. An alternative approach is to use Photocopiable master 3CPM2.

2 Which is the Hardest Material?

Teaching Activities

Provide the pupils with a range of materials suitable as covering in a classroom or entrance hall.

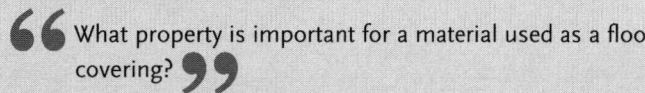 What property is important for a material used as a floor covering?

Make a list of the ideas. Hopefully they will suggest that the material should wear well or be hard. Tell them they are going to test the materials to find the most hardwearing.

Ask the pupils to suggest how a floor covering could be damaged. Ideas will probably include: things get dropped on the floor – we don't want it to dent; things rub against the floor (like shoes and bags!) – we don't want it damaged.

Ask:

How could you test the materials?

How can you make your test fair?

The 'dent' test can be accomplished by dropping a hard or heavy object down a cardboard tube onto the material. The object could be dropped once, or several times, and the material examined for damage.

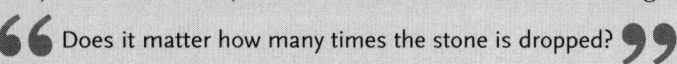 Does it matter how many times the stone is dropped?

The 'rub' test can be accomplished by using a hard material, such as a stone, small rock, or sandpaper and rubbing it against the surface. Remind the pupils about fair testing:

How many times should it be rubbed?

The pupils should be encouraged to make predictions.

Which material do you think will be the hardest? Why?

Pupils should be encouraged to support their predictions, e.g. 'Our tiles at home don't get scratched.'

They should then carry out their tests and answer the following about the results:

Has the same material come out best in both tests?

If your tests give different orders of hardness, how could you decide which material to choose?

Encourage the pupils to create a rating system using numbers or stars. The best material is the one with the highest number or star total.

Pupil Consolidation

Ask the pupils to list properties other than hardness, that are important in choosing a floor covering.

Ask the pupils to make a list of other items in a house or school which need to be hardwearing.

 **Timing**

2 hours

 Resources

- samples of floor covering: wood, carpet, plastic tiles, ceramic tiles
- cardboard tube (from kitchen roll), hard/heavy object such as a stone
- hard object for rub test, e.g. stone, brick, sandpaper

Key words

hardwearing   prediction

property

⚠️ **Safety**

The 'dent' test will need to be done carefully to prevent dropping the hard object onto fingers. Assess the risk and decide on the level of supervision needed. Similar precautions will be needed with the 'rub' test.

Pupil materials

3C 21 Pupil's Book page 21 prompts pupils to explain simple hardness tests.

Vocabulary

dragster

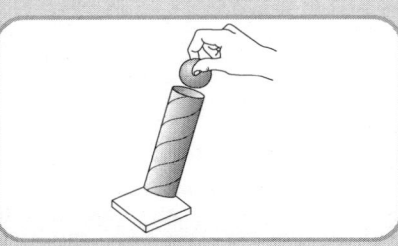

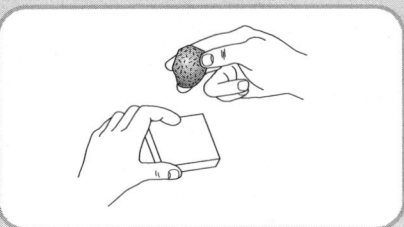

3 Which is the Best Paper Towel?

⏱ Timing
1½ hours

✏ Resources
- at least three different types of kitchen roll, paper towels or paper handkerchiefs, cut into 5 x 5 cm squares
- saucer or plastic tray – measuring cylinder or container which can measure a fixed amount of liquid
- squared paper for drawing bar charts

Key words
absorb   property

strength

Pupil materials

3C 22

3C 23

Pupil's Book pages 22 and 23 prompt pupils to answer questions about absorbent and packaging materials.

Teaching Activities

The pupils will be familiar with this type of investigation as it is similar to that used in Activity 2.

66 What properties should a paper towel have? 99

Ideas could include: it has to soak up liquid quickly; it has to soak up a lot of liquid; it has to be strong when wet.

Ask the pupils how they could find out which type of paper towel is the best for soaking up a liquid.

66 How could you measure how much liquid has been soaked up?
How can you make your test fair? 99

An easy way is to cut up the different samples into 5 cm squares, and pour a fixed amount of water into a saucer or a plastic tray.

66 How many squares are needed to soak up all the water? 99

The pupils will need to ensure that each square is soaked before adding another. You will need to experiment beforehand with the volume of liquid soaked up by a number of squares. The squares needed should be in the range 1–10 (10 sheets for the least absorbent material).

The pupils should compare at least three different makes of paper towel/kitchen roll. The results could be displayed in a bar chart. Pupils who find this difficult could stick the correct number of squares onto a large chart for display. The pupils should be encouraged to explain what they have found out, and to decide which is the best paper towel.

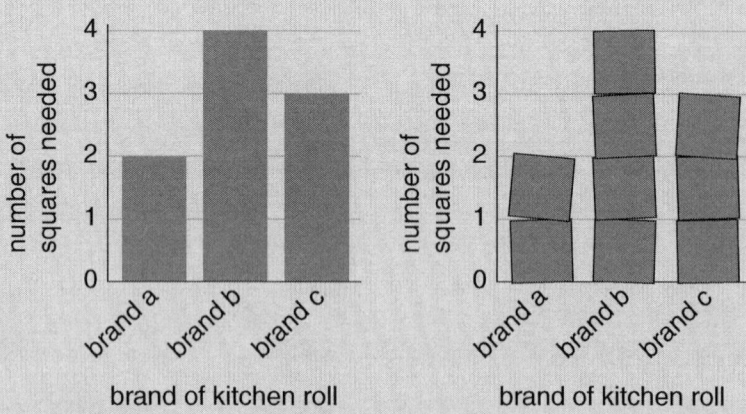

Pupil Consolidation

How could you find out how much liquid a bathroom sponge could hold? Write about what you would do and what you would measure.

4 Which is the Best Packaging Material?

Teaching Activities

Present the pupils with the following problem:

- **Context:** A relative, who lives in a different country, loves eating meringue nests but cannot buy them in her local shops. You decide to send her one by post.

- **Conditions:** It will have to travel many miles, mixed in with all sorts of parcels and letters. You don't want it to break in the post.

- **Task:** What would be the best way of wrapping it up?

Give the pupils some rules so that the 'parcels' can be made and then tested fairly. For example, you may give each group a box of the same size (a shoe box or preferably something smaller) and ask them to pack the meringue inside the box.

They will then need to decide how to test the boxes in transit. Be careful, you don't want all the meringues to break! Dropping boxes two or three times from a fixed height might be appropriate.

You may wish to restrict how much material they can use, and how many different types of material.

Ask the pupils what sort of property the wrapping material should have.

 Should it be hard or soft?

Should it be flexible or rigid?

Show the pupils a range of possible packing materials, and then let them choose. Ask them to justify their choices.

Once the meringues have been packed, the packages need to be tested. This is best done with the whole class together.

After testing, the pupils open their packages and the meringues are put on display for judging.

Pupil Consolidation

Look at the drawing of the different packaging materials. Why do you think they are used as packaging materials? Do they all have something in common?

Timing

1½ hours

 Resources

- small meringue nests, small boxes big enough to hold a meringue and some packing (e.g. tea bag boxes)
- a range of packaging material including polystyrene pieces, 'bubble wrap', shredded paper, newspaper, fabric samples etc. Sellotape, scissors

Key words

flexible   property

rigid

 Safety

Care should be taken if polystyrene pieces are used. The pupils must be warned not to put the pieces in their mouths.

Pupil materials

3C 22	Pupil's Book pages 22 and 23 prompt pupils to answer
3C 23	questions about absorbent and packaging materials.

5 Which Substances Melt?

Teaching Activities

This activity explores the melting points of substances. Changes of state are considered in detail in Unit 4D. Start a discussion by asking the questions:

❝ What happens when an ice cube warms up?

Why is butter or margarine kept in the fridge? ❞

Show the pupils a range of different substances.

❝ What will happen to these substances if they are heated?

Will they melt? ❞

Ask them to make predictions. Use the word 'temperature', for example:

❝ Will the chocolate melt if the temperature is increased? ❞

Provide the pupils with different substances in aluminium foil cases and allow them to float the cases on some hot water in a bowl. Ask them to observe the substances carefully.

❝ Are any of them beginning to melt?

Are there any that are not changing at all?

What happens when they are taken away from the hot water? ❞

The water will cool down quickly and so the pupils will need to be well organised.

Pupil Consolidation

Why did you use cases made from a metal (aluminium)?

What does the word 'reversible' mean? Write a sentence about your experiment. Use the word reversible in your sentence.

Timing
1½ hours

Resources
- aluminium foil cases
- samples of chocolate, butter, sugar and salt
- water bowls, access to hot water

Key words
conductor	melting
reversible	temperature

Safety
Care will be needed with the hot water. Boiling water from a kettle can be mixed with some cold water to give a suitable temperature.

Pupil materials

3C 24	Pupil's Book pages 24 and 25 prompt pupils to identify materials which melt and
3C 25	those which do not.

Vocabulary
occur (verb)

6 Key Activity:
Which is the Strongest Paper to Use for Paper Bags?

Previous Experience:

The pupils will need to have:

- used a ruler to measure in centimetres;
- had experience of fair testing;
- drawn bar charts, with help if necessary.

Which of the types of paper will make the strongest paper bags? The pupils need to compare at least three different types of paper.

Provide strips of paper, a range of small masses (weights) and some string. Ask pupils how they could test how strong the paper is. Give them some time to try out their ideas. Bring the class back together and share the ideas. It may be necessary to give them some hints or even discuss a particular approach with them. A useful hint is that a hole punch can be used to make a neat hole near the bottom of the strip through which the string can be tied. Try out beforehand the weight needed to tear or break the paper. This will give an idea of how narrow the strips need to be. (You will be surprised how difficult it is to break paper!)

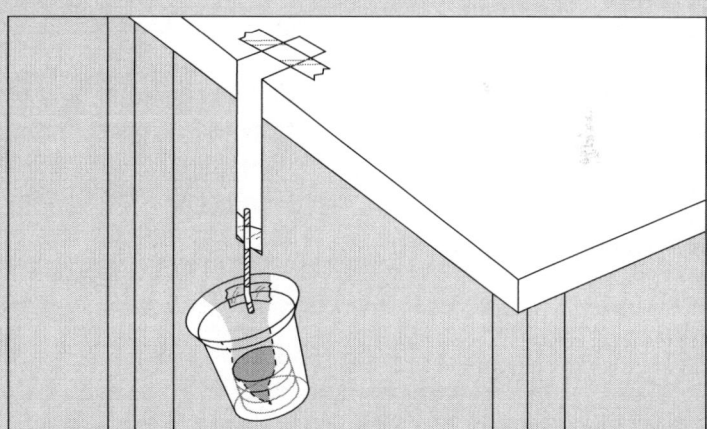

Give pupils Photocopiable master 3CPM3 and ask them to complete the planning section.

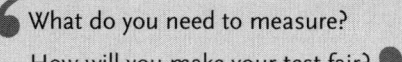 What do you need to measure?
How will you make your test fair?

They can then get on with the experimental work. Provide them with samples of the different papers, but don't cut them into equal-sized strips. It is important that the pupils realise this themselves.

Finally the pupils should complete the remainder of their record sheet (3CPM3) and, with help if necessary, draw a bar chart.

 **Timing**

2 hours

 **Resources**

- different samples of paper: some could be from paper bags, others could be chosen because they are not very strong – one of the samples should be cut into strips
- hole punch
- yoghurt pots, string and Sellotape
- 100 g masses or equivalent

Key words

prediction   mass

 **Safety**

There could be a risk of weights falling onto pupils' feet, etc. Try to choose a thin enough strip of paper so that it will tear before the weight is too great (aim for 500 g maximum).

Pupil materials

Photocopiable master provides a writing frame to guide the pupils' investigation of the strengths of different types of paper.

Assessment

The Assessment Pointers for Sc1 illustrate the possible levels of attainment in the context of the Key Activity.

Assessment Pointers for Sc1

Level	Planning Pupils can:	Obtaining and Presenting Pupils can:	Considering and Evaluating Pupils can:
2	make suggestions, with prompting, as to how the masses can be added to the strips of paper;	make observations such as, 'The white paper tore before the others did';	compare findings with, expectations, e.g. 'I thought the brown paper would be best'.
3	put forward ideas, without prompting, as to how the types of paper can be tested;	carefully add the 100 g masses one at a time to the paper strip until it breaks;	give a conclusion such as, 'The white paper was the strongest, then the brown paper and last was the green paper'.
4	plan a test using strips of paper the same length and thickness and add the masses in the same way;	draw a bar chart to show the mass needed to tear each piece of paper;	link the conclusion to a scientific idea, e.g. 'the white paper did not have any fibres'.

Pupil materials

End of Unit Question
Photocopiable master prompts pupils to identify the property of a material which makes it suitable for a particular use.

Mark Scheme

Question	Answers
1a	light
1b	burns
1c	does not bend easily
2	you can see through it (transparent) it is waterproof/it is strong

The Assessment Pointers for Sc3 illustrate how evidence from responses to questions and tasks in the Pupil's Book and on the Photocopiable masters can be related to the different levels of attainment.

Assessment Pointers for Sc3

Level	Evidence	Typical Outcome Pupils can:
2	Characteristics of Materials – Pupil's Book page 19	give a reason for using various materials on a bicycle;
	Materials in School – PM1	give a reason for the choice of a material for making something used in school.
3	Materials in the Home – PM2	give two reasons why a material is chosen for making a particular object;
	Materials for Purpose – PM4	give two reasons why glass is used in windows.
4	Materials Which Melt – Pupil's Book page 25, questions 1 and 2	name substances which melt easily and those which do not.

Key Ideas for Teachers

There are three main types of rock: igneous, sedimentary and metamorphic. Over millions of years these different types can be converted into each other through a process known as the rock cycle. Igneous rock is formed from magma that has erupted from the Earth's crust, usually from a volcano as lava. Over time igneous rock is worn away by the processes of weathering and erosion, creating small fragments of rock. These are transported by wind and water, eventually finding their way into rivers and the oceans. Sedimentation and cementation occurs, eventually forming sedimentary rock. If either igneous or sedimentary rocks are forced back into the mantle of the Earth (for example, in a process known as subduction) the intense heat and pressure can convert them into metamorphic rocks.

Type of rock	Appearance	Examples
igneous	hard, contains crystals of different minerals	granite, basalt
sedimentary	formed in layers, tends to be crumbly, fossils common	limestone, sandstone
metamorphic	crystals often distorted, fossils rare	marble, slate

Permeability depends on how much the particles of rock or soil pack together.

Key Ideas for Pupils

- to compare everyday materials on the basis of their properties;
- to describe and group rocks and soils on the basis of characteristics, including appearance, texture and permeability;
- that solid particles of different sizes, e.g. those in soils, can be separated by sieving.

These learning outcomes illustrate how the key ideas for pupils can be matched to different levels of attainment. They can also be used to check the level of demand of an activity.

Timing
10 hours

Glossary of terms

igneous	a rock formed from volcanic lava
manufactured	artificially made – to produce in quantity
metamorphic	a rock, initially igneous or sedimentary, that has been subjected to heat and pressure
natural	found in nature
permeability	the ability of water or air to make its way through the substance
sedimentary	a rock formed by deposition of rock fragments followed by cementation

Starting points

Pupils should be familiar with the following ideas:
- materials can be sorted into groups on the basis of simple properties;
- common types of material include metal, plastic, wood, paper and rock, and that some of these materials are found naturally.

Learning Outcomes

Pupils can:

Level 2	• name one or two different kinds of rock, for example, chalk and marble; • name soil types, for example, sand and clay; • recall that rocks are naturally occurring materials;	• state that rocks can be found in the ground, often covered by soil; • make simple observations.
Level 3	• name and describe the characteristics of several types of soil or rock; • explain that rocks are used for different purposes;	• state that soil is made from rock; • put forward ideas without prompting.
Level 4	• describe, with precision, the differences between rock samples, using terms such as layers and crystals; • explain in simple terms how the structure of a soil sample can be used to explain its permeability;	• use a simple key to identify different types of rock; • explain results obtained in an investigation.

The Assessment Pointers on page 38 show how these levels of attainment can be interpreted in the context of the specific activities used in the unit.

3D Rocks and Soils

1 Rocks as Natural Materials

Timing
1½ hours

Resources
- rock samples to include: granite, limestone (chalk), marble, slate, sandstone – a local monumental stone mason will have samples if you have difficulty getting them
- other natural materials such as coal and wood
- manufactured materials to include: brick, concrete (breeze block), iron, plastic
- samples of different types of soil (sand, clay, peat)

Key words
manufactured   natural

Pupil materials

3D PM1 Photocopiable master prompts pupils to research how some common manufactured materials are made.

3D 26 **3D 27** Pupil's Book pages 26 and 27 ask questions about natural and manufactured materials.

ICT Opportunity
opportunity for research

Teaching Activities

The purpose of this activity is to assess the pupils' existing knowledge, which can then be developed in the rest of the unit.

Depending on the local environment, it may be useful to take the class out to look at the types of 'rocks' around the school. Alternatively a display of rocks and other naturally occurring materials could be made available in the classroom.

The classification of naturally occurring or manufactured rock is not as simple for pupils to grasp as it may seem. For example, pieces of brick are often found in the ground; a polished piece of marble is not found in the ground, although marble itself is. If the material has only been shaped or polished it is classified as naturally occurring. Alternatively if it has been made from a number of ingredients it is manufactured, e.g. a brick. Pupils may not know that plastic is manufactured.

Tell the pupils they are going to learn about rocks and soils. Show them a sample of a naturally occurring rock such as chalk or granite, and a sample of a manufactured 'rock' such as a brick or a piece of concrete. Ask them what the differences between the samples are. If they describe the observable differences, encourage them to use a range of suitable vocabulary. Emphasise the classification as natural and manufactured.

 Could you find both of them in the ground?

If you had lived in the Stone Age do you think you could have found both in the ground?

One of them has been made by people – it has been manufactured. Which one do you think it is?

Which of the other materials do you think are natural?

What do you think the manufactured materials are made from?

How do you think they are made?

Where do you think soil comes from?

What is soil made from?

Ask them to do some research using books, CD-ROMs and other resources to find answers to some of these questions.

Pupil Consolidation

Some important materials are obtained from minerals.

What does the word mineral mean? (Use a dictionary.)

What is the name of a mineral that iron is obtained from?

2   Examining Rocks

Teaching Activities

Provide the pupils with samples of different types of rock (labelled A, B etc.). Ask them to use a hand lens to describe the appearance of the rock samples. Encourage the pupils to make accurate observations. Give them a list of prompt questions, for example:

> What colour is each rock?
>
> What is the texture? (Is it hard or soft?)
>
> Does the rock have crystals?
>
> Does the rock have layers?

Explain the terms 'crystal' and 'layer'. Crystals are like pieces of glass – they glisten in the light. (Crystals tend to form when molten rock cools down. If it cools too quickly the crystals tend to be small; if it cools slowly the crystals tend to be large). Layers are like lines in the rock. (Layers are characteristic of sedimentary or metamorphic rocks.) Show the pupils some rocks with crystals and some with layers. Examples of these are given in the Pupil's Book, page 28.

Provide samples of the same types of rock in different sizes. In this way, you can check that the pupils understand that different-sized pieces are still made of the same material. Pebbles, stones and rocks are all rocks!

Pupil Consolidation

Provide the pupils with a simple key and ask them to find out the names of the rocks you have given them.

Timing

1¹/₂ hours

Resources

- samples of rock as in Activity 1
- hand lenses

Key words

crystal   layer

Pupil materials

3D PM2

Photocopiable master prompts pupils to make observations of different rock samples and to try and identify the type of rock using a key.

Timing

2 hours

 Resources

- samples of different types of rock, e.g. chalk, sandstone, granite, marble
- sandpaper or a stone/pebble
- dropping pipette

Key words

non-permeable   permeable

 Safety

Pupils should be warned to carry out the hardness test with care. They should rub the rock slowly and not trap their fingers.

 ICT Opportunity

opportunity for research

3   Comparing the Hardness and Permeability of Rocks

Teaching Activities

Provide the pupils with four samples of rock. Explain that you need to decide which is the best rock to make a monument or gravestone.

Remind the pupils that the rock will be outside, constantly battered by wind and rain. Hopefully they will suggest that the rock should be hard and waterproof. Tell them that if water can seep into a rock it is permeable. If water cannot seep in then it is non-permeable.

Ask the pupils to look at their rock samples, using hand lenses if appropriate. Ask them to make two sets of prediction:

- an order of hardness (hardest to softest);
- an order of permeability (least permeable to most permeable).

Ask them what they have looked for before making their predictions. Once they have written down their predictions, discuss the tests:

1   Hardness test. A simple 'rub' or 'scratch' test can be used. The former is safer. Pupils could rub the rock with a course grade sandpaper. Alternatively they could use a stone or pebble. (See unit 3C.)

2   Permeability test. A dropper can be used to add one drop of water to the rock sample. Does some of the water soak in or does it stay as a droplet on the surface?

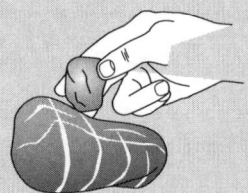 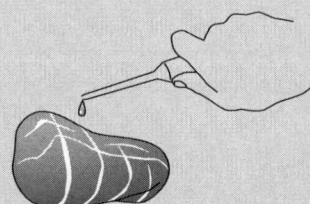

Ask the pupils to test the rock samples and to produce an order of hardness and an order of permeability. Then ask them to choose the best rock for making a monument or gravestone.

 Why have you chosen that rock?

Was it the best on both tests?

Were your predictions correct?

Pupil Consolidation

Ask the pupils to write about their experiment and what they have found out.

Use reference books or CD-ROMs to find out what monuments or gravestones are made from.

4 Research into Different Types of Rock

Teaching Activities

The particular focus of this activity will depend on the resources available, for example, books, CD-ROMs, videos, Internet access etc. It will be most important to provide a series of specific questions in order to encourage the pupils to find information and extract that which is relevant.

The pupils could do some research on a named example of a rock, such as granite, basalt, limestone etc., or on igneous, metamorphic or sedimentary rocks.

For their named example, or type of rock, they should investigate and record answers to the following questions:

1 What does it look like? Can you make a drawing of it?

2 Where in the world is the rock found?

3 How was the rock made?

4 What is the rock used for?

Encourage the use of a table like this:

	Granite	Limestone
What does it look like?		
Where in the world is it found?		
How was it made?		
What is it used for?		

Timing
1¹/₂ hours

Resources
- reference books, access to library, computer, Internet as appropriate
- writing frame to guide research task

Pupil materials

3D 28 Pupil's Book page 28 provides guidance to research a rock sample.

3D 29 Pupil's Book page 29 prompts pupils to identify some uses of common rocks.

Vocabulary
identify (verb)
ornament

ICT Opportunity
opportunity for research

Timing
1¹/₂ hours

Resources
- samples of sandy, clay and peat soil
- hand lenses
- large measuring cylinders or clear plastic beakers

Key words

air	clay
humus	particles
peat	sand

Safety
The pupils should wash their hands after completing this activity.

Pupil materials

3D 30 **3D 31** Pupil's Book pages 30 and 31 prompt pupils to explain how soils can be compared with a fair test.

Vocabulary
to depend on

5 Looking at Types of Soil

Teaching Activities

Explain that soil is made up of small fragments of rock.

 How do you think the small fragments may have been formed?

They have been formed by rocks rubbing together or by the wind and rain breaking pieces off the rocks.

Demonstrate how a sieve can be used to separate the different sizes of particles.

Provide the pupils with three different samples of soil: a sandy soil, a clay soil and a peat soil. Let them use hand lenses and make a list of their observations.

Demonstrate what happens when the soil is added to water. Use a large transparent beaker or measuring cylinder.

 What do you think are the bubbles rising to the surface?

Where have they come from?

What is the material that is floating on the surface of the water?

Why is this important?

In this way the pupils are introduced to the idea that air is trapped in the soil – that there must be gaps between the soil particles. Also plant material or humus is often mixed in with soil – it provides 'goodness' for the soil so helping things grow.

Pupil Consolidation

Ask the pupils to do a survey of the type(s) of soil found in the school grounds. Try and identify places where they will find different types. For example, flower borders will often contain peat, whereas other places might have sandy or clay soils. Give the pupils a simple map of the school site and ask them to mark where they find each type of soil.

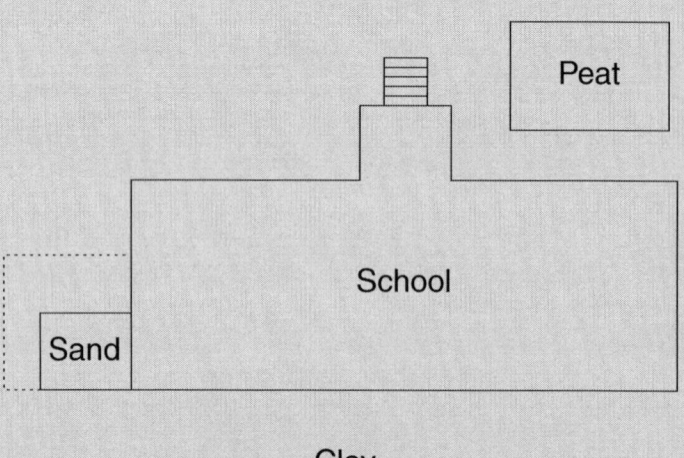

6 Key Activity:
Comparing the Permeability of Different Types of Soil

Previous Experience:

The pupils will need to have:

- measured the volume of a liquid using a measuring cylinder;
- made predictions supported with a reason;
- used simple tables for recording results.

Ask the pupils where puddles form when it rains.

> Do you ever see puddles on the grass or the soil?
>
> Why do you think puddles form there, but not in other places?
>
> Could it be due to the type of soil and how easily water finds it to drain through the soil?

Show them the three types of soil. Tell them they will test how easily water passes through the soil (how permeable or how porous the soil is). You might then show them a container they could use to hold the soil in – a filter funnel or yoghurt pot with holes in the base.

> What will you do?
>
> What will you measure?
>
> How will you make sure your test is fair?

(You can give further hints here by asking how much soil they will use.)

soil

yoghurt pot (with holes in the bottom)

Let the pupils experiment briefly with one of the soil samples. Let them see how long the water takes to drain through. This should enable them to decide on the quantities of soil and water.

The soil must not be packed too tightly into the funnel or it will take a long time for the water to soak through. Equally the soil must be pressed down to stop water running down the side of the funnel.

Ask the pupils to complete the first part of the Photocopiable master 3DPM3 (planning section). Then allow them to carry out the investigation before completing the rest of the sheet.

 **Timing**

2 hours

 **Resources**

- soil samples: sandy soil, clay soil, soil with high humus content (it is advisable to make up your own sample with high humus content)
- filter funnels
- measuring cylinders
- timers

Key words

permeability   porous

 Safety

The pupils should wash their hands carefully after completing their investigation.

Pupil materials

3D PM3

Photocopiable master provides a writing frame to guide pupils' approach when comparing different soil samples.

Assessment

The Assessment Pointers for Sc1 illustrate the possible levels of attainment in the context of the Key Activity.

Assessment Pointers for Sc1

Level	Planning Pupils can:	Obtaining and Presenting Pupils can:	Considering and Evaluating Pupils can:
2	make suggestions with help as to how they could compare the different soil samples;	make observations such as, 'The water went through the peat soil much quicker than through the clay soil';	compare findings with expectations, e.g. 'I was right, the clay was very slow!'.
3	put forward ideas without prompting as to how the soil samples can be compared;	measure the volume of water accurately using a measuring cylinder and with help make sure the test is fair;	make simple conclusions such as, 'The water went quickest through the peat soil, then the sand and then the clay'.
4	plan to use the same depth of soil and the same amount of water to ensure the test is fair;	measure the volume of water that passes through each soil sample in 1 minute;	explain the results in terms of the gaps between the soil particles.

Pupil materials

End of Unit Question

Photocopiable master prompts pupils to interpret information from a scratch test to answer questions about rocks.

Mark Scheme

Question	Answers
1	chalk
2	no
3	steel could not scratch flint
4	granite or flint

The Assessment Pointers for Sc3 illustrate how evidence from responses to questions and tasks in the Pupil's Book and on the Photocopiable masters can be related to the different levels of attainment.

Assessment Pointers for Sc3

Level	Evidence	Typical Outcome Pupils can:
2	Rocks and Soils – Pupil's Book page 27, questions 1 and 2 Looking at Rocks – PM2	give a reason why coal is a natural material whereas glass is not; describe the colour of a number of rock samples and whether they are rough or smooth.
3	What are Rocks Used For? – Pupil's Book page 29 Looking at Rocks – PM2	identify the type of rock that is used for various purposes; describe rocks in terms of crystals and layers.
4	Looking at Rocks – PM2 Looking at Rocks – PM2	compare the crystal and layered structures of different types of rock; use a key to identify different types of rock.

Key Ideas for Teachers

Magnetic materials contain particles which can align themselves in such a way that they display magnetic properties. The end that points to the Magnetic North Pole is called the 'north-seeking pole' (N–pole). The other end is called the 'south-seeking pole' (S–pole). The simple law of magnetism is that unlike poles attract; like poles repel. Only a few materials can be used to make magnets, or are attracted to magnets. It is a common misconception to think that all metals are magnetic. In the pupils' experience only objects made of iron or steel will be magnetic. Drink cans are made from steel or aluminium. They can be identified before recycling by using a magnet. The most powerful magnets are electromagnets, where an electric current can generate massive magnetic forces.

Forces are measured in newtons (N). A force of 1N will hold a 100 g mass against the force of gravity. Newtonmeters (or forcemeters) contain a spring. A spring is an elastic material, it will return to its original length after stretching, providing it isn't stretched beyond its elastic limit. For an elastic material the force is directly proportional to the extension (if the force is doubled the extension will be doubled).

Key Ideas for Pupils

- the forces of attraction and repulsion between magnets, and the forces of attraction between magnets and magnetic materials;

- that objects are pulled downwards because of the gravitational attraction between them and Earth;

- that when objects, such as a spring or a table, are pushed or pulled, an opposing pull or push back can be felt;

- how to measure forces and identify the direction in which they act.

These learning outcomes illustrate how the key ideas for pupils can be matched to different levels of attainment. They can also be used to check the level of demand of an activity.

Timing

9 hours

Glossary of terms

elastic limit	the greatest stress a material can be subjected to without permanent distortion
electromagnet	a powerful magnet produced using an electric current
gravity	the force that attracts everything to the centre of the Earth
magnetic materials	materials which are attracted to a magnet
N–pole	the north-seeking pole of a magnet
S–pole	the south-seeking pole of a magnet

Starting points

Pupils should be familiar with the following ideas:

- the movement of familiar things, for example, cars speeding up, slowing down, changing direction;
- pushes and pulls are examples of forces;
- when things speed up, slow down or change direction, there is a cause, e.g. a push or a pull.

Learning Outcomes

Pupils can:

Level 2	• describe what happens when some materials are put near to a magnet; • use a newtonmeter to find out which is the bigger of two forces;	• make simple observations.
Level 3	• measure forces accurately in Newtons; • recognise that a force acts in a particular direction. Describe the direction of forces between magnets and when a spring is being stretched;	• make a simple solution.
Level 4	• explain that gravity is a force that acts towards the centre of the Earth and recognise the consequences of gravity in everyday situations;	• make a series of measurements to find a pattern.

The Assessment Pointers on page 45 show how these levels of attainment can be interpreted in the context of the specific activities used in the unit.

3E Magnets and Springs

1 Forces

Teaching Activities

The purpose of this activity is to assess what the pupils can remember from Key Stage 1 about forces and to emphasise the importance of the force of gravity in many everyday situations.

Start with an object on the table, such as a piece of Plasticene. Tell the pupils that you want them to apply a force to the Plasticene.

 What can you do to put a force on this Plasticene?
How many different types of force can you use?

The pupils should come up with words such as pull, push, squash, squeeze, twist, stretch and throw.

Give the pupils a series of drawings showing everyday things in motion. Ask the pupils to name the main type of force and to add an arrow to each for the direction of this force. At this stage concentrate on the main force – there should only be one arrow on each drawing. (The idea of balanced and unbalanced forces does not now need to be covered until Key Stage 3.)

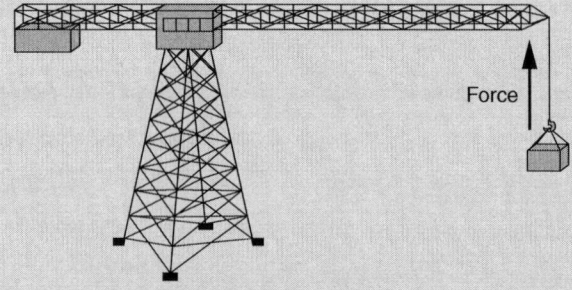

Force

Go over the examples with the pupils. Talk particularly about the situations where gravity is the main force.

 What is gravity?
What does it do?

Use the pupils' answers to make a concept map.

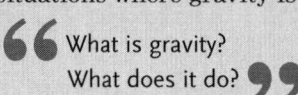

Concept map

a force
a pull .... makes things fall
gravity
things always fall .... the Moon is pulled
to the ground   makes things   by the Earth
                       run down hill

Pupil Consolidation

Use reference books, CD-ROMs etc. to find out six facts about gravity.

Is it true that there is no gravity on the Moon? What can you find out?

Timing
2 hours

Resources
- Plasticene

Key words

force	gravity
pull	push
stretch	squash
squeeze	twist

Pupil materials

3E PM1 Photocopiable master prompts pupils to identify the direction and type of different forces.

3E 32
3E 33 Pupil's Book pages 32 and 33 prompt pupils to identify some effects of forces and the direction of the force of gravity.

ICT Opportunity
opportunity for research

2 Magnets and Magnetic Materials

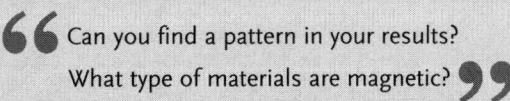

Teaching Activities

The first part of this activity links closely to Activity 1 in Unit 3C. If Unit 3C has been covered a quick recap will be needed.

Provide each pupil, or group, with a bar magnet. Ask the pupils to find five magnetic objects and five that are non-magnetic. Ask them to make a list of the magnetic and non-magnetic objects, and the materials they think that each object is made from.

 Can you find a pattern in your results?

What type of materials are magnetic?

If the pupils say that all metals are magnetic, show that metals such as copper and aluminium are non-magnetic. Stress that only objects made from iron or steel are magnetic.

Show the pupils some magnetic games or novelty items which contain magnets. It is always interesting to show two circular magnets in a transparent cylindrical tube, arranged so that they repel each other. Give the pupils as wide a variety as possible of different types of magnet, including bar, horseshoe and circular magnets etc.

Do the magnets always stick together (attract each other)?

When do the magnets stick together and when do they push apart (repel)?

Explain that the magnet has two ends, or poles – the north and the south. North poles are usually coloured red and south poles blue.

What happens when the two red ends are pushed together?

What happens when the two blue ends are pushed together?

What happens when a red and a blue end are pushed together?

Can you make up a simple rule for magnets?

Pupil Consolidation

Find out as many different uses for magnets as you can.

What is an electromagnet? What is it used for?

 Timing

1½ hours

 Resources

- bar magnets and an assortment of other types of magnets, for example, horseshoe, circular etc.
- any games with magnets (e.g. Brio train set) or novelties which make use of magnets (e.g. fridge badges etc.)

Key words

attract   magnet

pole   repel

 Safety

The pupils should not put their magnets near to tape recorders or computers.

Pupil materials

3E PM2	Photocopiable master prompts pupils to identify situations where magnets attract and repel each other and gives some uses of magnets.
3E 37	Pupil's Book page 37 prompts pupils to identify magnetic materials.

Timing
2 hours

Resources
- an assortment of bar magnets (new and old) and other magnets, horseshoe, circular etc.
- paperclips (small)

Key words
attract   magnet

Pupil materials

3E 34   3E 35   Pupil's Book page 34 to 37 prompt pupils to identify magnetic materials and interpret information from an experiment to compare the strengths of different magnets.

3E 36   3E 37

ICT Opportunity
opportunity for research

3   Which is the Strongest Magnet?

Teaching Activities

A simple way to test the strength of a magnet is to see how many paperclips it can hold, with the paperclips linked together. Using small paperclips should give a range of results with up to about eight clips being held by the strongest magnet.

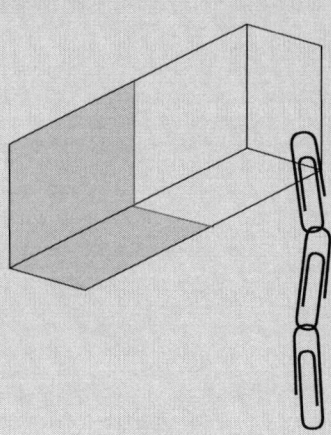

Tell the pupils that their task is to find out which is the strongest magnet. Demonstrate how they can use paperclips to test each magnet. The pupils should test at least three magnets and preferably more. Ask the pupils to design a table to record their results in.

 Which magnet is the strongest? How do you know?

Which magnet is the weakest? How do you know?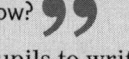

When you have discussed their results, ask the pupils to write a conclusion.

Pupil Consolidation

By using books, CD-ROMs and any other sources of information find out:

- how magnets get damaged;
- how to make an iron nail into a simple magnet.

LAR

fer ID: 2124323
m ID: 25167835
ce Paid: £0.25

od
ge Books
nuel Holmes
-1-04-004-002 15057
ence Directions – Year 3 Teaching
e: Practical guidance on planning,
anising and teaching h
11/2023 01:56:55

15057

LAR

4 Stretching Springs and Rubber Bands

Teaching Activities

Give each pupil a rubber band and ask them to stretch it carefully without breaking it.

 What can you feel?

Can you feel a force trying to pull the rubber band back to its starting length?

Draw a diagram using arrows to show the two forces: the force caused by hands pulling the rubber band; the force of the rubber band trying to return it to its original length. Show that different thicknesses of rubber band need different forces to stretch them.

Demonstrate similar forces using a spring. Some springs can be stretched very easily, others need much greater forces to stretch them. Use a spring to lift an object. Point out that the spring stretches but when the object is removed the spring returns to its normal length.

 What happens to the spring if I try and lift a heavier object?

Explain that a spring can be used to make a force measurer known as a newtonmeter. Talk about the newton as the unit of force used by scientists.

Ask the pupils to use a newtonmeter to find the force needed to lift various objects. Ask them to choose ten objects to lift and to record their results in a table. Stress that it is important not to try and lift an object that is too heavy. This would stretch the spring so much that it would not return to its original length. (Most newtonmeters do not allow the spring to be over-stretched.)

Discuss the results with the pupils.

 Which object took the greatest force to lift it?

Which object took the smallest force to lift it?

Which object has the greatest weight?

What is the name of the force which pulls objects towards the ground?

Pupil Consolidation

Explain how a newtonmeter works.

Timing
1½ hours

Resources
- an assortment of rubber bands
- an assortment of springs
- newtonmeters

Key words

gravity	heaviest
lightest	newton
newtonmeter	weight

Pupil materials

3E PM3
Photocopiable master prompts pupils to weigh a range of objects with a newtonmeter.

3E 38 **3E 39**
Pupil's Book pages 38 and 39 prompt pupils to interpret the results from an experiment on the strength of springs.

5 Key Activity:
Investigating Catapults

Previous Experience:

The pupils will need to have:

- made supported predictions;
- planned fair tests;
- measured distances in centimetres;
- made conclusions from results and supported them with scientific knowledge.

The idea is to use a rubber band to 'fire' an object along the ground and find out what pattern exists between the amount of stretch on the band, and the distance travelled by the object.

The rubber band can be stretched over the front legs of a chair, pulled back different distances and then released. The distance travelled by the object can then be measured. It is important to try this before the lesson and choose an object that the band will hit easily when released. A small wooden brick might be appropriate or a multilink cube. Results are often better if the band is released to hit the cube, rather than pulling the cube back with the band. Plenty of room will be needed to prevent groups firing cubes onto the same part of the floor.

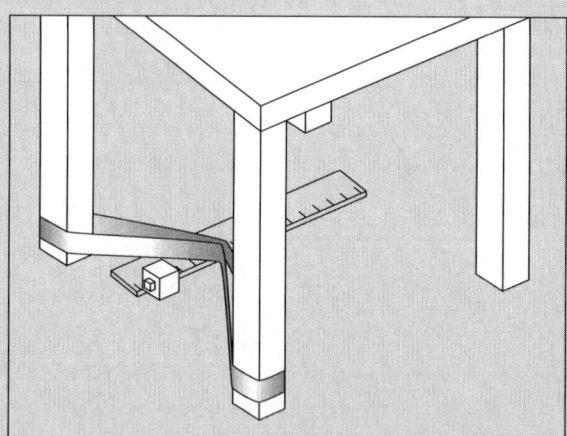

Give the pupils time to practise the technique and to get a feel for how far the rubber band needs to be pulled back. Then ask the pupils to complete the planning section of the Photocopiable master 3EPM4. Allow the pupils to perform the investigation, encouraging each group to take at least four different measurements.

They should record their results in the table.

In the plenary ask the pupils what they have found out.

 Is there a pattern between how far the band is pulled back and how far the cube travels?

Can you explain this pattern?

Timing

2 hours

Resources

- a selection of rubber bands
- objects to act as 'projectiles', for example, multilink cubes, small wooden bricks etc.
- rulers and tape measures

Key words

force	distance
stretch	

⚠ Safety

The pupils should be warned not to stretch the rubber bands too much as they will break and exert a big force on someone's hand!

Pupil materials

3E PM4 Photocopiable master provides a writing frame to guide the investigation of a catapult.

Assessment

The Assessment Pointers for Sc1 illustrate the possible levels of attainment in the context of the Key Activity.

Assessment Pointers for Sc1

Level	Planning Pupils can:	Obtaining and Presenting Pupils can:	Considering and Evaluating Pupils can:
2	make suggestions, with prompting, as to how they can investigate how the amount of stretch of the band affects the distance the object travels;	make simple observations, for example, 'The cube has gone further this time';	compare findings with expectations, e.g. 'I didn't think it would go that far!'.
3	put forward their own ideas for finding the relationship between amount of stretch and the distance travelled by a cube;	measure the distance the band is pulled back, and the distance travelled by the cube to the nearest centimetre;	make a simple conclusion, e.g. the more the band was stretched the further the cube went.
4	plan a fair test using the same rubber band, with the same cube in the same starting position each time;	measure the distance travelled by the cube for at least three different values of the amount the band was stretched;	provide supported conclusions, e.g. the more the band was stretched the greater the force on the cube and the further it went.

Pupil materials

End of Unit Question Photocopiable master asks questions about magnets and the direction of a magnetic force.

Mark Scheme

Question	Answers
1a)	bar magnet
1b)	it held the most paperclips
2	arrow pointing from paperclip to magnet
3	plastic is not magnetic

The Assessment Pointers for Sc4 illustrate how evidence from responses to questions and tasks in the Pupil's Book and on the Photocopiable masters can be related to the different levels of attainment.

Assessment Pointers for Sc4

Level	Evidence	Typical Outcome Pupils can:
2	Magnets and Magnetic Materials – Pupil's Book page 37, question 1	identify steel and iron as magnetic materials;
	Using a Newtonmeter – PM3	say which object is the heavier by using a newtonmeter.
3	Things in Motion – PM1	correctly show the direction of the force acting in at least five of the drawings;
	Magnets – PM2	correctly identify the situations where the bar magnets will attract each other and those where they will repel each other.
4	Forces – Pupil's Book page 33, question 2	identify gravity as the force acting and correctly show the direction in which it acts;
	Springs – Pupil's Book page 39, question 2	identify the pattern in the results and make a prediction based on this pattern (predicts that spring B will stretch 10 cm).

Key Ideas for Teachers

The ultimate source of light is the Sun. Light is able to travel in straight lines and it can travel through empty space.

In diagrams, lines known as rays show the direction in which the light is travelling.

Shadows are formed when an opaque object is placed in front of the light source and effectively blocks the path of the rays. If the light comes from a single point, for example, a tiny light bulb, the shadow will have very sharp edges. If the light comes from a source that is more spread out the shadow has a fuzzy edge.

Light can be reflected from different kinds of surfaces. If the surface is uneven (microscopically) images cannot be seen as the light is scattered in all directions. If the surface is very smooth, as in a mirror, then an image is reflected back along its path and an image is seen.

Prisms can also be used as mirrors. They are most useful when they do not split the light into the colours of the rainbow, for example, when they are used in a periscope.

As light travels only in straight lines, lenses can be used to refocus an image on a point so that it can be seen. This is the way spectacles work. Light appears to bend when it moves through a different medium, for example, from air to glass, or air to water. This is because the rays travel at different speeds through different media.

Key Ideas for Pupils

- that light travels from a source;
- that light cannot pass through some materials, and how this leads to the formation of shadows;
- the Sun appears to change position during the day, and how shadows change as this happens.

These learning outcomes illustrate how the key ideas for pupils can be matched to different levels of attainment. They can also be used to check the level of demand of an activity.

Timing

12 hours

Glossary of terms

image	the visual impression of an object produced by a lens or mirror
ray	the term used to describe the direction a beam of light is travelling, e.g. in a diagram
refraction	the angle of change in direction of a ray of light as it passes through one medium to another
shadow	the shade cast by an object stopping beams of light

Starting points

Pupils should be familiar with the following ideas:

- light is needed in order to see;
- there are many different light sources;
- the main source of light is the Sun.

Learning Outcomes

Pupils can:

Level 2	• describe how the shape of a shadow is similar to the object causing it;	• describe how the shadows caused by the Sun change over the period of a day; • describe some materials that block the light.
Level 3	• explain that a shadow is formed when a light source is blocked; • use the terms translucent, transparent and opaque to accurately describe the features of some materials;	• select a range of materials to test based on their physical properties.
Level 4	• explain that shadows change as a result of the movement of the Earth in relation to the Sun;	• explain that even translucent objects form shadows; • make a suggestion of how to improve their experiment.

The Assessment Pointers on page 54 show how these levels of attainment can be interpreted in the context of the specific activities used in the unit.

3F Light and Shadows

1 Light and Dark Concepts

Teaching Activities

Talk to the pupils about what they know of light and dark. They will have studied this previously in unit 1D Light and Dark. Ask them questions like:

> Is it always light during the day?
>
> Is it ever light at night?
>
> Where can light come from?

Allow the pupils to tell you and the rest of the class their experiences of very light and dark places. Some pupils may have visited caves and grottos while on holiday. Provide them with Photocopiable master 3FPM1 to use as the basis of a concept map describing what they know about light and dark. Explain that the words already on the map are only there to start them off. They should feel free to cross out the words provided and replace them with words of their own. They should draw lines to make links with words and include drawings.

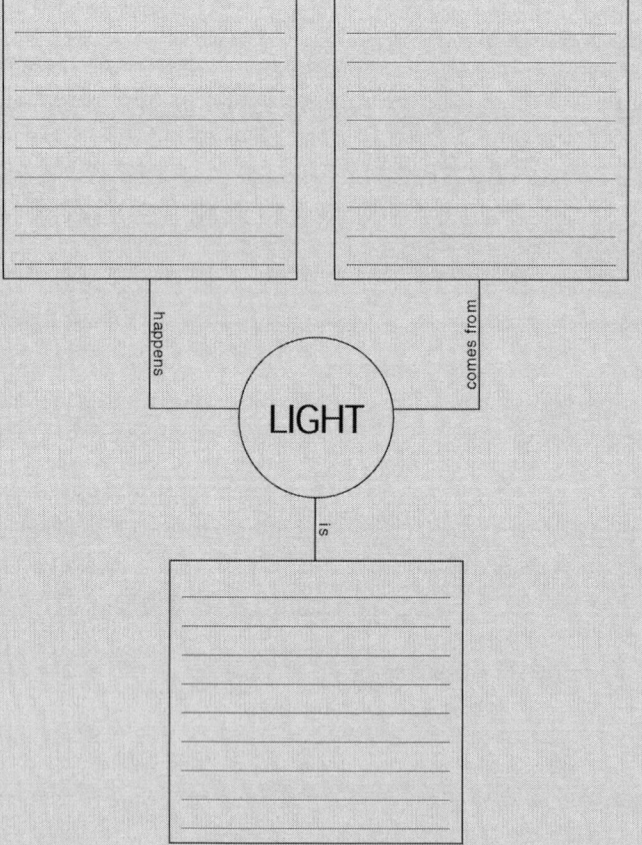

When the pupils have completed their maps they should explain to other pupils the links that they have made. The maps should be displayed in the classroom and referred to throughout the unit.

 **Timing**

2 hours

 Resources

- paper
- coloured pens

Key words

dark	lamp
light	shade

Pupil materials

3F PM1 Photocopiable master provides a blank concept map on light.

2 Shadow Formation

Teaching Activities

Ask the pupils what they understand by the term shadow. Gather all their ideas. Ask who used the word shadow on their concept map. Challenge pupils to explain what they mean by the word.

> How can we make a shadow?
>
> What do we have to do to make a big shadow?
>
> Can we make a shadow that is coloured?

Gather the pupils' ideas and then give them access to the resources. Instruct them to find as many different ways of making shadows as possible. Allow at least 15 minutes for the pupils to explore.

Stop the class and ask them what they have found out. At this point many pupils will be convinced that they can make a coloured shadow. Demonstrate with the OHP or a slide projector the beam of light produced. Putting a cardboard cylinder in front of the light source will let pupils observe that light travels in straight lines. Place a comb with large teeth in front of the beam. Ask the pupils to explain what they see.

Pupil's Book page 41 examines large and small shadows.

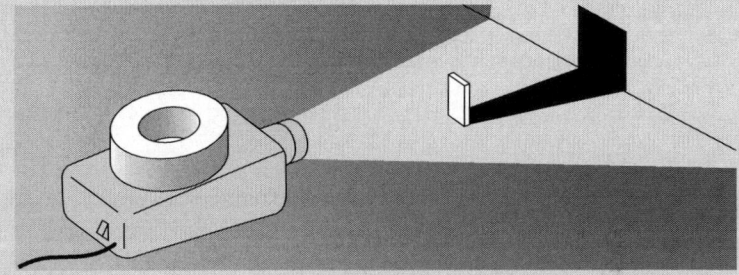

Establish that where the light goes between the teeth it can be seen on the screen, but where the teeth block the light a shadow is formed.

If a piece of coloured acetate is placed over the comb the pupils will observe that the shadows of the teeth remain the same but the light travelling through the spaces is coloured. Explain that these are not true shadows because the light is able to pass through the coloured filter and this shows on the screen.

Pupils should write up their experiments and include drawings.

Pupil Consolidation

Produce an illustrated shadow poem using the sentence starter from the word shadow.

The next two activities provide early experiences for unit 5E Earth, Sun and Moon.

Timing

2 hours

 Resources

- torches
- overhead projector
- slide projector
- fabric samples
- coloured acetate type material (sweet wrappers)
- white board or large sheets of paper to reflect shadows onto
- comb

Key words

block   light beam

shadow

 Pupil materials

| 3F 40 | Pupil's Book pages 40 and 41 prompt pupils to experiment with light to examine large and small shadows. |
| 3F 41 | |

3 Body Shadows

Teaching Activities

Note: This activity requires a sunny day to be successful. It is also best carried out in the morning. If this is not possible leave at least two hours between looking at the shadows.

Ask the pupils:

 What do you think is the largest light source?

They may mention football stadium lights and fireworks. Explain that these are all very bright sources of light, but the biggest one is the Sun.

Put the pupils in pairs and give them a piece of chalk. Take the pupils outside onto the playground and ask one of each pair to stand so that they make as big a shadow as possible. Their partner should draw around the shadow. They should also draw around the feet so that the orientation of the shadow can be revisited later. The shadows should be named. The pairs should then swap over and the second partner challenged to make as small a shadow as possible. Again the shadow should be drawn around and labelled. (Pupil's Book page 42 illustrates pupils measuring their own shadows.)

As the pupils are making their shadow drawings ask them to feel where the Sun is in relation to where they are standing. For example:

 If a big shadow is made, is the Sun directly on your back?

Take the pupils to another part of the playground. Ask them to make obscure shadows by twisting their bodies and then draw around them. If you have a Polaroid or digital camera take some photos. (There are links here to Art and the work of David Hockney.)

Take the pupils back into the classroom and ask:

 Predict what you think your shadow will look like in the afternoon.

Photocopiable master 3FPM2 will provide a framework for this. Explain to the pupils that they will look at their shadows again in a couple of hours, and make additional drawings to see how they have changed.

Return to the shadows later in the day and realign pupils to their original position. They should record how the shadows have changed (there is space on 3FPM2 for this).

Pupil Consolidation

Looking at the obscure shadow pictures that they made, see if it is possible to recreate the patterns. Try again at the same time on the following day. Discuss with the pupils why they think that the shadows have changed.

Timing
2 hours

Resources
● chalk
● camera

Key words
behind	long
overhead	shadow
short	small
Sun	wide

Pupil materials

3F PM2 Photocopiable master provides a framework for pupils' predictions.

3F 42 **3F 43** Pupil's Book pages 42 and 43 show pupils measuring their shadows.

Vocabulary
glance

4 Sun Movement

Teaching Activities

Recap the work on shadows from last lesson and ask the pupils:

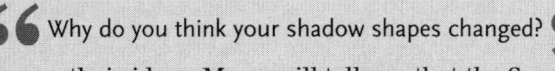 Why do you think your shadow shapes changed?

Discuss their ideas. Many will tell you that the Sun moves around the Earth during the day. The concept, that it is in fact the Earth moving, will not be fully understood at this stage.

Demonstrate with a model figure (or doll) and a powerful torch how long and short shadows are made. Ask:

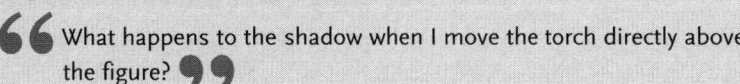 What happens to the shadow when I move the torch directly above the figure?

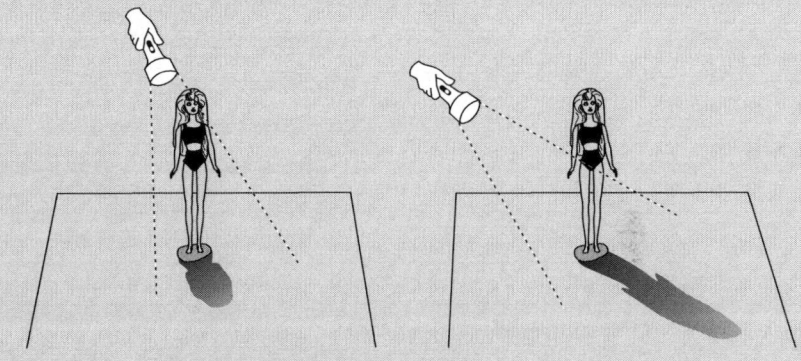

Let the pupils explore using a similar set up. If figures are not available a matchstick is a good substitute.

Show the pupils some cut-out circles about 10 cm across. Ask them to look out of the classroom window and, while not looking directly at the Sun, point out where it is. Stick the circle on the window at an appropriate point. Assign pupils to be in charge of placing other discs on the window at hourly intervals during the day.

If the Sun cannot be seen through the windows take the pupils outside and place a shadow stick on the playground. Mark around the base as the pupils did with their feet. Note the time of day and draw with chalk the length and orientation of the shadow. Return hourly and repeat the exercise.

Towards the end of the day the pupils should look at their results and explain what has happened. They should note that the shadows have changed direction, and the length has changed from long to short back to long again. Or they should note the discs on the window have moved across the classroom and have gone up and down the window.

Explain to the pupils that it is the Earth that is moving and the Sun that stays still. The shadow patterns are caused by the Earth moving around on its axis. These points will be built upon and extended in unit 5E.

Pupil Consolidation

Research using CD-ROM or the Internet how different civilisations have used the Sun to tell the time by the formation of shadows.

Timing

2 hours

Resources

- figure (doll)
- torch with a powerful beam
- paper circles about 10 cm in diameter
- Blu-Tack
- shadow stick (broom handle)

Key words

longer · movement
shadow · shorter
time

ICT Opportunity

opportunity for communication and data search

3F Light and Shadows

Timing
2 hours

Resources
- lots of different materials to cut up, e.g. paper, card, greaseproof paper, clingfilm, transparent coloured film, fabric samples
- torches
- screens
- dowel
- scissors

Key words

clear	fuzzy
opaque	shadow
transparent	translucent

Pupil materials

3F 46	Pupil's Book pages 46
3F 47	and 47 illustrate children putting on a shadow puppet performance.

5 Shadows in the Classroom

Teaching Activities

Explain to the pupils that, while they have been having fun with shadows, they have been learning quite a lot. Ask them to look at their concept maps again:

 Have you changed your mind about anything you wrote on your concept map?

They should amend their maps accordingly.

Ask:

Can you think of any rules to explain the way shadows are formed?

Hopefully they will think of the following: that the light source must be behind; big shadows are made when the light source is close to the object.

Show them the materials available and explain that you want them to either make up a story, or use one of their favourite published ones, to make a shadow puppet story. The story should last for five minutes and demonstrate what they know about shadows. Challenge them to make their characters different by using sharp and fuzzy edges to their puppets. They should also be able to make the characters different sizes by moving the puppets nearer or further away from the screen.

The pupils should plan their shadow puppet show by writing the script and drawing what they are going to do with the characters at the side.

When all the pupils have performed their shows to the rest of the class, ask:

 How many different ways did you find to make your puppets?

Show them a piece of card, some greaseproof paper, and clear plastic. Remind them that they may have used special words for the materials during 1D Light and Dark at Key Stage 1. Establish the words **transparent**, **translucent** and **opaque**. Ask the pupils if they used examples of these materials for their shadow puppets. They should identify on their puppets where they used the materials and what effects they had on the shadows.

Explain that they are going to use their knowledge of these materials in the next investigation. Pupil's Book pages 46 and 47 show pupils putting on a shadow puppet performance.

Pupil Consolidation

The pupils could research the way in which magic lantern shows were established in bygone years (link with History).

6 Key Activity:
Transparency Investigation

Previous Experience:
The pupils will need to have:

- made simple predictions;
- recorded their results in simple tables;
- talked about results of an experiment.

Show the pupils a range of materials (see Resources). Explain that you are interested to know which materials would be good to make a dark den for the Key Stage 1 pupils to play in. The den should have a window that could be covered up with a curtain.

Tell them that they need to predict which materials would stop the light most effectively. They should also predict which materials should be used for the window and its curtain. Show them a torch with a bright beam and explain that you want them to devise a test for the materials that they have been given. Demonstrate how to make the test fair by holding the torch a given distance from the material, and a pupil a set distance away from the material to see if they can see any of the light through the material.

Higher attaining pupils could try to quantify the amount of light that passes through different materials, with the torch at different distances away.

If senses are available, pupils could try to quantify the amount of light able to travel through a material. The pupils should plan and carry out their tests. Photocopiable master 3FPM3 will provide a format for this.

At the end of the experiment discuss with the pupils what they have found out about transparent, translucent and opaque materials. Link this to previous work on shadows and ask them to state which type of material makes the best shadow. They should decide that opaque materials make the best shadows. More able pupils will be able to tell you that even translucent materials make some shadow but that the shadow is not as apparent as the opaque ones.

Pupil's Book pages 44 and 45 consolidate pupils' understanding of the terms transparent, translucent and opaque.

Timing
2 hours

Resources
- materials used in Activity 5
- torches
- rulers

Key words

dark	distance
light	opaque
through	transparent
translucent	

Pupil materials

3F PM3	Photocopiable master provides a format for carrying out tests.

| 3F 44 | Pupil's Book pages 44 and 45 examine materials that are opaque, translucent and transparent. |
| 3F 45 | |

ICT Opportunity
sensing

Assessment

The Assessment Pointers for Sc1 illustrate the possible levels of attainment in the context of the Key Activity.

Assessment Pointers for Sc1

Level	Planning Pupils can:	Obtaining and Presenting Pupils can:	Considering and Evaluating Pupils can:
2	suggest testing a number of different materials to see if the light will pass through;	make simple observations about the material: 'It lets light through';	describe materials that block the light.
3	suggest testing a selected range of materials based on their physical properties;	measure approximate distances during their tests;	identify simple patterns in their data, e.g. 'most fabrics let light through a bit'.
4	decide to measure the distance of the material from the torch and the distance from the material of the person;	make a series of observations of the materials, moving them different distances from the light beam;	suggest that their experiment could have been improved by using a light sensor to be more accurate, or using a much darker room so that differences in light levels are easier to see.

Pupil materials

3F PM4

End of Unit Question
Photocopiable master asks pupils to explain how shadows are formed.

Mark Scheme

Question	Answers
1	front of puppet and screen
2	the stick blocks the light from the Sun and the shadow is formed
3	shadow will be shorter because the Sun appears higher in the sky (nearly overhead)

The Assessment Pointers for Sc4 illustrate how evidence from responses to questions and tasks in the Pupil's Book and on the Photocopiable masters can be related to the different levels of attainment.

Assessment Pointers for Sc4

Level	Evidence	Typical Outcome Pupils can:
2	Body Shadows – PM3	describe how shadows caused by the Sun change.
3	Light and Shadows – Pupil's Book page 40, questions 1, 2 and 3	explain that shadows are formed when a light source is blocked.
4	Shadows Outside – Pupil's Book page 42, questions 1, 2 and 3	explain how the change in shadows caused by the Sun arise from the movement of the Earth.

Party Menu

You are having a party for your birthday at the local swimming pool. After swimming you are going to have some food. Design a menu for yourself and ten friends for the party. Remember to make the food healthy and colourful.

My healthy birthday party menu

Starters

Main courses

Sweets

Snacks and drinks

Explain to a friend why you have chosen the various foods.

Which of these foods should you eat only a little of?

Dental Decay

Write a leaflet to be placed in your local dental surgery. The leaflet should point out the dangers of dental decay.

fold

HEALTHY MOUTHS

fold

Remember to make your leaflet as exciting to read as possible and full of information.

The following letter is from Bright Smile Incorporated. They would like you to carry out some research into their toothpastes. Read the letter before starting your investigations.

Bright Smile Incorporated
Complete Oral care

Dear Research Team,

As you are aware, we are a leading manufacturer of toothpastes, toothbrushes, floss and mouthwashes. We have a dedicated team of researchers and technologists who ensure that only products of the highest quality reach customers.

As part of a new advertising campaign we are asking teams of Junior researchers to test out the claims we make for our products. We will then be confident that we know what nine out of ten people prefer!

Please help us by investigating how well two of our toothpastes work on sticky foods such as Mars Bars and jam. The ingredients in our toothpastes are identical with one exception. One paste has the added ingredient of bicarbonate of soda. We suggest you use the standard white tile technique for your tests.

We would really like to hear your opinion on the following:
- Which toothpaste is best?
- Does the amount of water used have any effect?
- Do any of the toothpastes reduce the need for scrubbing?

We understand you will not all want to investigate the same question, but we appreciate conclusions on all aspects of our products.

We look forward to hearing your results.

P. Etearf

Dr. Pearl Etearf
Senior Research Chemist

De Montfort Industrial Park, Beacon Way, Cheshire RC4 0TW
Tel 01834 639 265 Fax 01834 678 945 www.brightsmile.co.uk

Clean Teeth

I will use:

- scratched white tiles
- melted Mars Bar
- toothbrush
- toothpaste
- toothpaste containing bicarbonate of soda
- water
- timer.

I want to know if

I will find out what I want to know by

I know that my test will be fair because

I think that I will know what will happen. I think that

I think this because

End of Unit Question

Adapted from Key Stage 2 SATS Test A Question 1a, 1998

3A
PM5

Teeth

The dentist gave this child a tablet which dyes the plaque on the teeth.

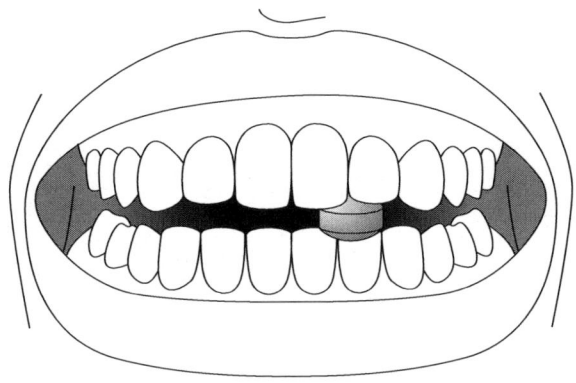
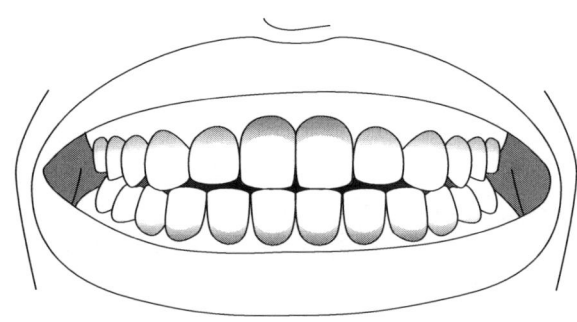

Before using the coloured dye   *After using coloured dye*

Plaque leads to tooth decay.

1 a) What can you do to stop plaque building up on your teeth between visits to
   the dentist?

_____

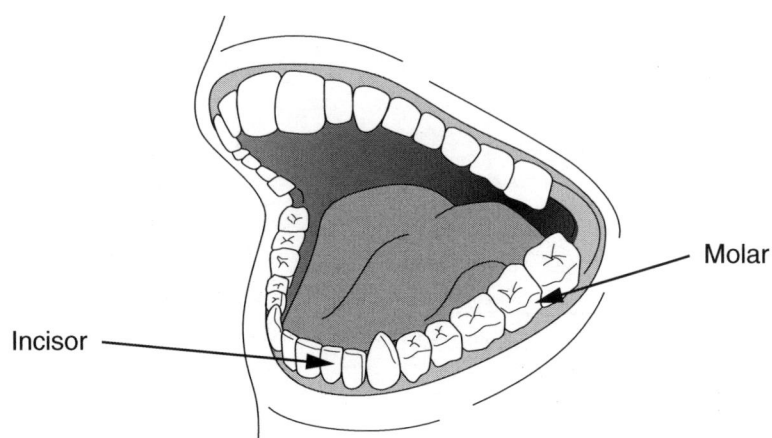

Molar

Incisor

   b) Different types of tooth do different jobs when we bite food. Look at the
   picture. What jobs do molars and incisors do?

_____

_____

Investigating Plant Growth

A number of plants have been left to grow.

Make a drawing of what they look like now in the boxes (remember to count the number of leaves).

Date: _____

1	2	3	4	5

Look at the plants again after one week.

Draw what they look like now.

Date: _____

1	2	3	4	5

What do you think they will look like in another week?

_____

How did you make sure that your experiment was fair?

_____

What do you think plants need to help them grow well?

_____

 © HarperCollins*Publishers* Ltd 2000

Plant Grower's Guide 1

Your task is to make a Plant Grower's Guide Book for other pupils in school to use.
Use the beginning of these sentences to help you.

1 The things that you need to help plants grow are…

2 The first thing that you must do is…

3 Then you must…

4 You will know that your plants are healthy because…

5 You can tell that they are growing by…

6 Finally, you can…

Remember to make your guide colourful by adding pictures to illustrate your text.

Plant Grower's Guide 2

On this side of your guide add any information that you have found out about the way plants are adapted to grow in different places.

These examples will give you some clues.

Example of a plant grown in hot places.

Example of a plant grown in wet places.

Example of a plant grown in woodland.

Example of a plant grown near the sea.

© HarperCollins*Publishers* Ltd 2000

How plants feed

1 What do plants need to grow well?

   Tick **two** boxes.

   ☐ pots   ☐ insects   ☐ worms

   ☐ water   ☐ rocks   ☐ air

2 Animals take in their food.

   Plants do not.

How do plants obtain food ?
_____
_____
_____
_____

3 Which of the following sentences are true?

   Tick **two** boxes.

   The roots of a plant take in water.   ☐

   The roots of a plant make seeds.   ☐

   The roots make food for the plant.   ☐

   The roots anchor the plant.   ☐

   The roots of a plant make it green.   ☐

Materials in School

Walk round your school.

Look carefully at what materials things have been made from.

Why do you think certain materials have been used?

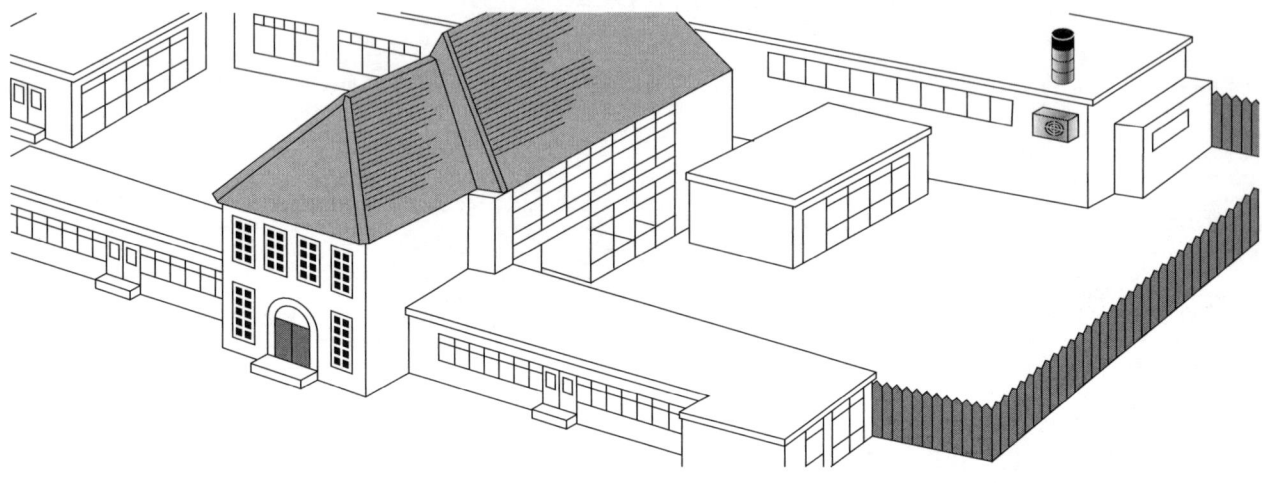

Complete the table below.

The first row has been filled in for you.

Choose properties such as:

hard, soft, flexible, strong, rough, smooth, light, heavy, transparent, magnetic.

Something found in the school	What material has been used to make it?	Why has the material been chosen for this use?
entrance door	wood	hard and strong

Materials in the Home

For each object shown in the table below write down what material you think it is made from.

Give a reason why that material has been chosen to make the object.

Write your answers in the table.

The first one has been done for you.

> Choose properties of the material.

Object	Material the object is made from	Why is this material chosen?
	wool	soft and smooth

Which is the Strongest Paper?

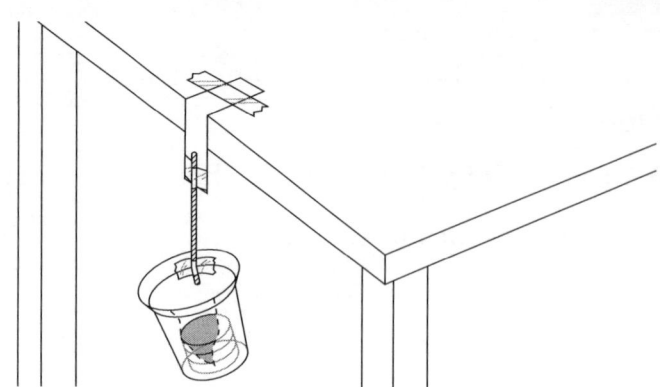

You are going to investigate which paper is the strongest.

You will probably test your paper using equipment like that shown in the diagram.

Planning

Which paper do you think will be the strongest? Give a reason for your answer.
What will you need to measure?
How will you make your test fair?

Results

Write your results in the table.

Type of paper	Weight needed to break it (g)
_____	_____
_____	_____
_____	_____
_____	_____

What have you found out?

Which paper was the strongest?	Is this what you predicted?

Draw a bar chart of your results. (Do this on a separate piece of paper.)

Materials for Purpose

1 Tick **one** box to complete each sentence:

a) Plastic is used for trays because it

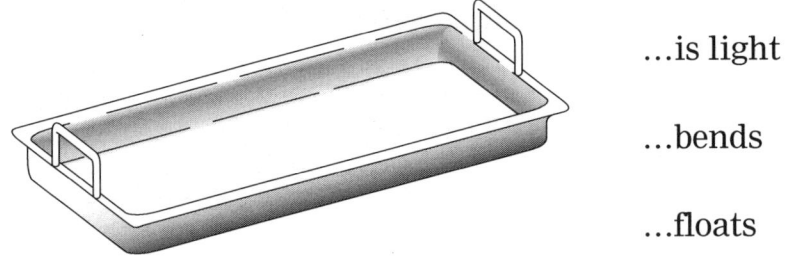

…is light ☐

…bends ☐

…floats ☐

b) Wood is used for matches because it

…floats ☐

…snaps ☐

…burns ☐

c) Steel is used for nails because it

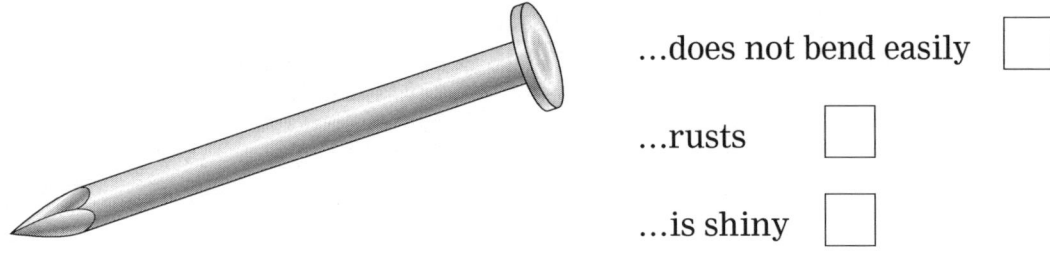

…does not bend easily ☐

…rusts ☐

…is shiny ☐

2 Different parts of the bus are made from different materials.

The windows are made from glass.

Write down **two** reasons why glass is a good material for making windows.

a) _____

_____

b) _____

_____

Some materials are natural – they can be found in the ground.

Write down the names of six natural materials:

1 _____   4 _____

2 _____   5 _____

3 _____   6 _____

Other materials are manufactured – they are made from other things. For each material write down in the table what it is made from.

Manufactured material	What it is made from?
plastic	
concrete	
brick	
steel	

© **HarperCollins**Publishers **Ltd 2000**

Looking at Rocks

Look carefully at the rock samples.

Complete the table.

	Rocks			
	A	**B**	**C**	**D**
Does the rock have crystals?				
What colour is the rock?				
Does the rock have layers?				
What is the name of the rock? (Use the key below.)				

This key can be used to find out the names of some rocks.

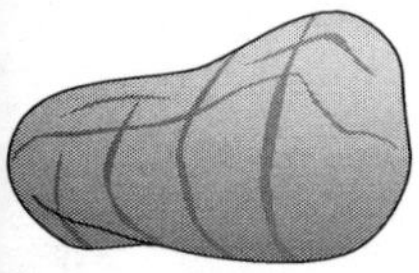

```
                    Does the rock have crystals?

            YES                              NO

      Is the rock white?            Does the rock have layers?

     YES          NO               YES              NO

    Marble      Granite           Slate           Chalk
```

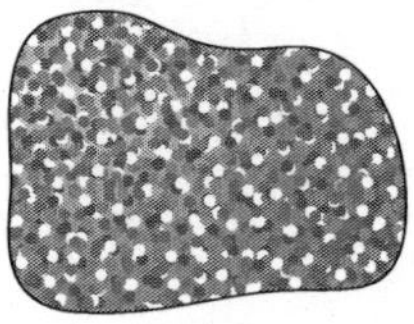

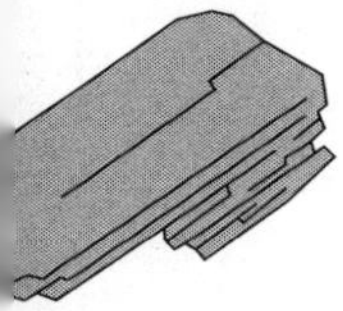

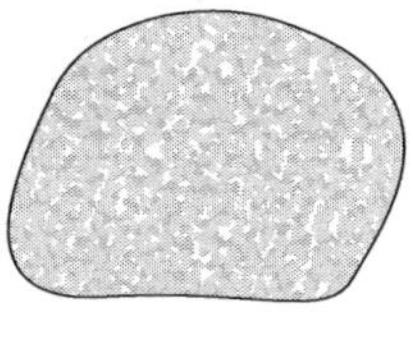

Comparing Different Soils

You are going to investigate which soil lets water soak through it the quickest.

You will probably test the soils using equipment like that shown in the diagram.

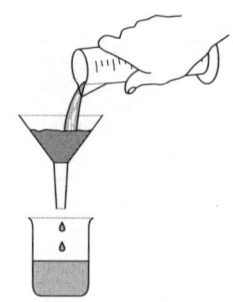

Planning

Which soil do you think the water will soak through the quickest? Give a reason for your answer.	
What will you need to measure?	
How will you make your test fair?	

Results

Put your results in the table.

Type of soil	Time taken for water to soak through (seconds)

What have you found out?

Which soil did the water soak through the quickest?	
Is this what you predicted?	

Draw a bar chart of your results. (Do this on a separate piece of paper.)

Comparing Different Soils

Jo and Kelly tried scratching rock samples with a fingernail and with steel.

A fingernail is quite soft. Steel is hard.

They recorded their results.

Rock	Scratched with:	
	fingernail	steel
chalk	✔	✔
flint	✗	✗
granite	✗	✗
sandstone	✗	✔

✔ = made a scratch   ✗ = did not make a scratch

1 Which is the softest rock in the table?

_____

2 Use the table to decide if steel is harder than flint. Tick **one** box.

☐ yes   ☐ no   ☐ maybe   ☐ can't tell

3 Explain your answer to question 2.

_____

_____

_____

4 Name **one** rock in the table which is harder than sandstone.

_____

Things in Motion

Look at the drawings of the moving things.

Name the main type of force shown, for example, pull, push, squash, squeeze, twist, stretch.

Draw an arrow to show the direction of the force.

The first one has been done for you.

FORCE

Type of force: __push__

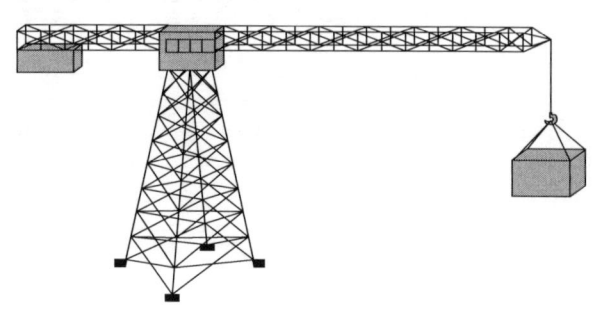

Type of force: _____

Type of force: _____

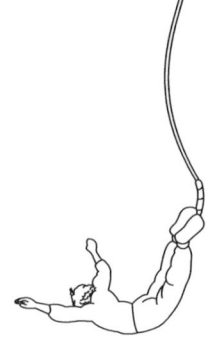

Type of force: _____

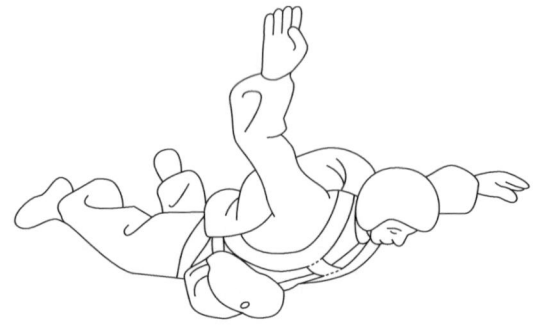

Type of force: _____

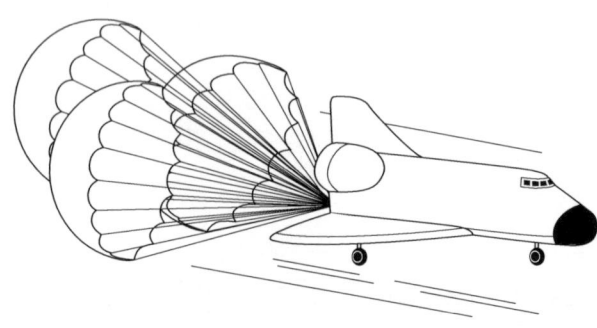

Type of force: _____

Magnets

For each drawing tick one box.

the magnets attract ☐

the magnets repel ☐

the magnets attract ☐

the magnets repel ☐

the magnets attract ☐

the magnets repel ☐

the magnets attract ☐

the magnets repel ☐

Make a list of some uses of magnets

1 _____

2 _____

3 _____

4 _____

What is an electromagnet? _____

_____

© **HarperCollins***Publishers* **Ltd 2000**

Using a Newtonmeter

Use your newtonmeter to lift some objects.

Write down the force needed in newtons.

Write your results in the table.

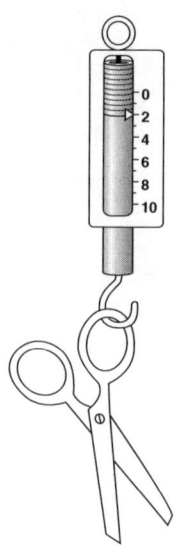

Name of object	Force needed to lift the object in newtons (N)

1 Which was the heaviest object?

_____

2 Which was the lightest object?

_____

Investigating Catapults

You are going to find out how increasing the amount of stretch on a rubber band changes how far an object can be 'fired'.

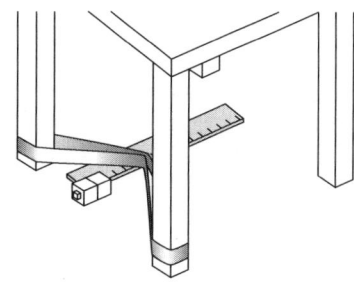

Planning

How do you think changing the amount of stretch will change how far the object is fired? Give a reason for your answer.
What will you need to measure in your investigation?
How will you make your test fair?

Results

Write your results in the table.

Amount the rubber band was stretched (cm)	Distance the object travelled (cm)

What have you found out?

What pattern can you see in your results?
Can you explain this pattern?

Magnets

1 Children tested the strength of three magnets by finding out how many steel paperclips each magnet held. They recorded their results.

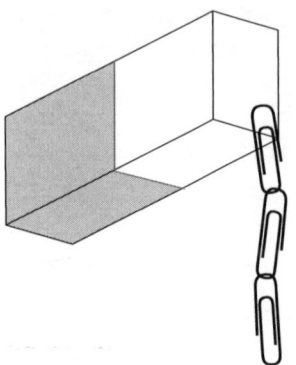

magnet	number of paperclips held
horseshoe	3
bar	8
round	5

Look at the results table.

a) Which is the strongest magnet?

_____

b) Explain how you decided which is the strongest magnet.

_____

_____

2 Draw an arrow on this drawing to show the direction of the magnetic force which holds the paperclips in this position.

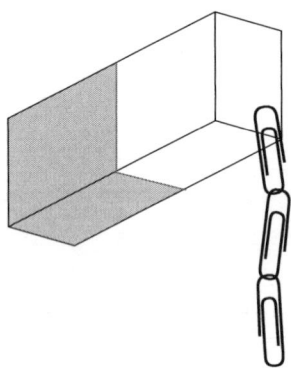

3 Explain why a magnet will not attract plastic paperclips.

_____

_____

_____

happens

comes from

LIGHT

is

Body Shadows

Fill in the following grid as you do your experiment.

Me and my shadow at _____ o'clock	What I think me and my shadow will look like at _____ o'clock	What my shadow looked like at _____ o'clock

This is what me and my funny shaped shadow looked like.

Transparency Investigation

My investigation to find the best materials to make a dark den

These are the materials that I will use.

_____

This is how I will set up my tests.

_____

I will make my test fair by

_____

These are my results.

Material	How well it blocked the light
_____	_____
_____	_____
_____	_____
_____	_____

My results tell me that the best material for the walls is

_____

because   _____

My results tell me that the best material for the window is

_____

because   _____

My results tell me that the best material for the curtains is

_____

because   _____

End of Unit Question

Adapted from Key Stage 2 SATS Test A Question 5, 1996, and Test A Question 7, 1998

3F PM4

Beryl and David have a torch and a shadow puppet. What does the light from the torch shine on?

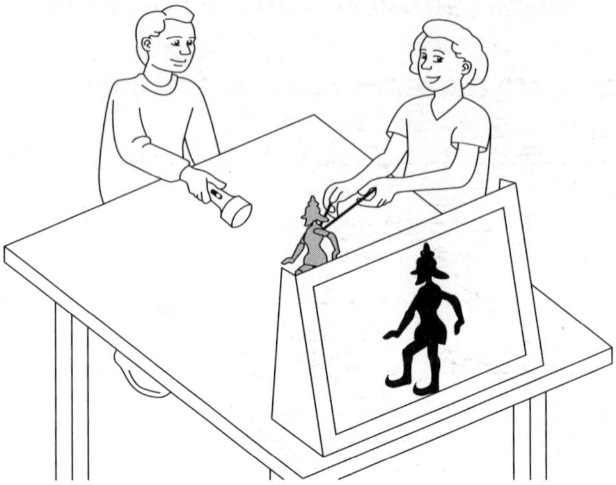

1 Tick **two** boxes.

the front of the puppet ☐

the back of the puppet ☐

the shadow of the puppet ☐

the screen ☐

The pupils then went outside and measured the length of a stick's shadow at different times of the day in summer.

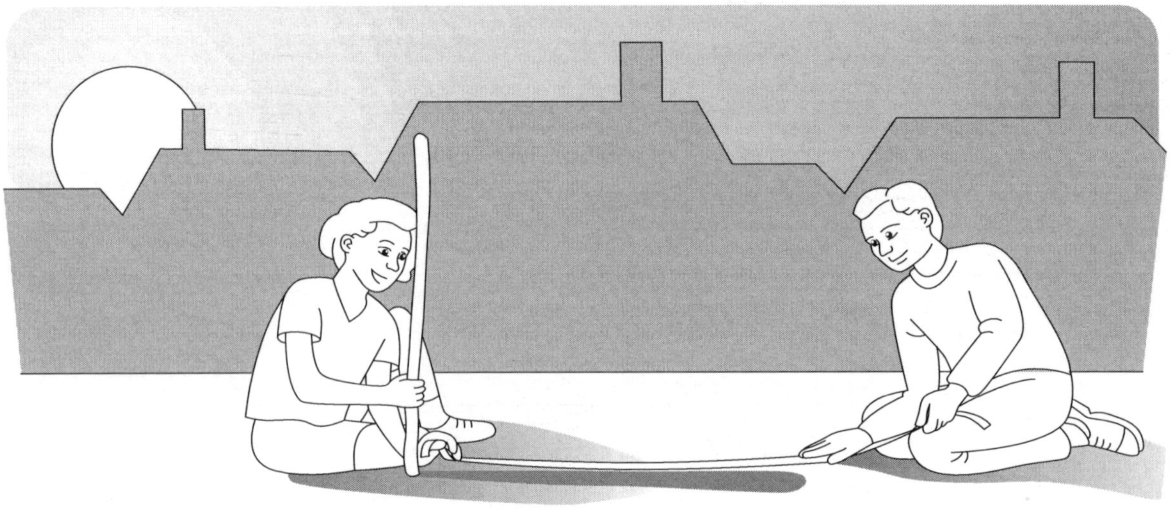

2 Explain how the shadow of the stick is formed.

____

____

____

3 At one o'clock in the afternoon the shadow has changed length. Will it be longer or shorter?

The shadow will be ______________________

Because ______________________

____

© HarperCollins*Publishers* Ltd 2000